1-19-72

The Consumer's Handbook II

The Consumer's Handbook II

100 Ways to Get
More Value for Your Dollars

By the Staff of

THE NATIONAL OBSERVER

DOW JONES BOOKS
PRINCETON, NEW JERSEY

Introduction

The business of living grows more complex despite all the labor-saving appliances and devices that fill our homes. The devices break and often there's no one to fix them. Inflation deflates the buying power of insurance or savings accounts. Those who turn to other investments may confront a confusing world of REITs or no-load mutual funds. Then, just as things settle down for the summer, one of the broods of 17-year "locusts" emerges and starts splintering the dogwoods.

Every week The National Observer, a newspaper published by Dow Jones & Co., publishes articles, columns, and items designed to make the business of living a bit easier or more pleasurable. Usually they combine specific suggestions on meeting problems with advice on where to get more detailed information.

Sometimes, though, an article's major function is to put the reader on guard by discussing a problem for which solutions are either difficult or yet to be found. August Gribbin's discussion of the mail-order industry is an example. **1680464**

The business of living involves many subjects and areas so the spectrum of articles in the book is broad. It ranges from a discussion of whether beer drinkers really can tell the difference between brands to choosing a homebuilder; from double-drug dangers to the workings of variable annuities; and from wig picking to vital information a woman needs quickly if her husband dies.

This volume contains the best of consumer-oriented articles appearing in The National Observer as the nation moved into the 1970s. Because the passage of even a few months brings many changes to the business of living, each article has been rechecked and, where necessary, brought up to date. Even so, some specifics may change between browsings, particularly those involving prices.

National Observer staff members, past and present, who have contributed to the book include: Mr. Gribbin, Morton C. Paulson, Ann M. Lancaster, Susan Abbasi and Marion Simon. This volume was edited by Walter A. Damtoft, news editor for consumer affairs.

We believe their efforts will make the business of living a little easier, a little more fun.

—THE EDITORS

Contents

Section I — Automotive

Section II — Education

Section III — Health and Safety

Section IV — Food and Household

Section V — Investing

Section VI — Recreation and Hobbies

Section VII — Miscellaneous

The Consumer's Handbook II

Reducing Auto Corrosion

STREET slush produced by snow- and ice-melting chemicals often makes car owners worry about rusted fenders. But road salts are only one major cause of corrosion. Humid ocean-side air and even polluted urban atmospheres also shorten the life of an automobile body.

Corrosion, then, should be a year-round concern of anyone who lives in an area where his vehicle is subjected to one or more of these harmful conditions.

Rust—more correctly called corrosion when referring to the deterioration of metals other than iron and steel—is formed from an electrochemical process that eats away metal. Moisture enables it to take place. Road salts, salt air, and industrial pollutants contain chemicals that accelerate corrosion. Heat also speeds up the process.

So high humidity, especially in warm climates or in heated garages, fosters corrosion. The presence of salt makes it worse. Road salts, in particular, help collect moisture and keep it in a liquid state below normal freezing temperatures. Dirt can trap moisture and keep it from evaporating.

Severe auto rust generally starts on inside surfaces where metal is unprotected by paint and moisture collects. In the north, where road spray is the chief culprit, corrosion usually starts underneath the car. In coastal or industrial areas, where chemical deposits from the air are to blame, corrosion begins on the top of the car.

Auto manufacturers have made efforts to reduce corrosion, especially among higher-priced models. They use corrosion-resistant zinc in galvanizing body steel and in primer paint. Most new car bodies are dipped entirely in primer paint; often they are electrically charged to make the primer coating cling more tightly. The use of rust-resistant metal coatings and alloys, as well as plastics, is increasing. Exterior paint has improved. Even body styling has been changed so that less moisture is trapped in vulnerable parts of the body.

Because of these advances, automobiles are becoming less prone to rust out. But along with the improvements have come more use of salt on highways and greater amounts of harmful pollutants in city air.

Anyone planning to drive a car on snowy streets may want to consider having a new car undercoated by the dealer. For $20 or $30—more for larger cars—the underside of the vehicle will be coated with a thick substance probably having an asphalt base. This coating, designed as much for soundproofing as for moisture protection, will help keep water, salt, and dirt away from the metal parts most susceptible to road spray. But it has a weakness: It tends to crack with age and in very cold weather, so it can let in corrosives and perhaps even trap them next to the metal.

Car owners who live in high-corrosion areas and who plan to keep their cars for more than three or four years may find it advantageous to have them rust-proofed. This involves more than just undercoating and costs more—$80 on the average and even more for large cars, such as station wagons.

Small holes are drilled in door bottoms and other enclosed areas so that a protective spray, usually with an oil-wax base, can be applied inside. Exposed surfaces also are treated. Spraying and drying a car takes a full day. Inspections are advised every year or two thereafter to find areas where the coating has worn off.

There are two rust-proofing franchises with garages in scores of cities across the U.S.—Ziebart and Tuff-Kote. Both offer money-back guarantees against rust coming through metal they have coated, provided the cars are brought in while less than three months old or with fewer than about 3,000 miles on them.

Some local independent garages will rust-proof automobiles for less than a franchised operator. Any amount of rust-proofing is likely to do some good, but a car owner should find out beforehand how extensive the treatment will be and whether the work will be guaranteed.

Even without rust-proofing or undercoating, a car can be guarded against rust by the owner's everyday maintenance. For maximum protection, follow these steps:

✔ Wash your car frequently.

✔ Keep the car cool and dry. Putting a wet car into a humid, heated garage, especially if salt has been deposited on the body, is asking for a corrosion problem.

✔ Check drainholes at the bottoms of doors and other enclosed areas to make sure they are open and let water escape.

✔ Stop exterior rust by keeping a good wax coating on the car and by touching up scratches and spots where stones or other car doors have chipped away paint. If however, an area is spotted with many small, brownish-red blisters, there is not much you can do from outside the car; that's rust coming from the inside.

How Gasoline Is Rated

HIGH-PERFORMANCE automobile engines require high-performance gasolines. But many dollars are wasted when a car owner buys a better-quality fuel than an engine can use advantageously.

The most common quality used in describing gasolines is octane, a measure of the fuel's ability to operate an engine without knocking. Few drivers know what octane their car needs; even fewer are aware of the octane rating of the fuel they buy.

Nobody, not even the manufacturer, can tell an automobile owner exactly what gasoline is needed for his car without extensive tests of various fuels in that particular vehicle. Successive engines from the same assembly line often have peculiarities that make the fuel requirements of one differ from another. Fuel needs also are affected by climate and differences in driving habits.

Why is octane so important, and just what does it measure?

As each spark plug ignites the compressed fuel-and-air mixture in an engine cylinder, the burning is even and relatively slow. The combustion creates pressure and heat. The pressure drives the piston down and powers the car; the heat is removed by oil and water jackets that surround the cylinder. Both heat and pressure are greater in today's high-compression engines.

If a fuel with too low an octane number is used, the heat and pressure from combustion will cause the still-unburned portion of fuel in a cylinder to explode suddenly rather than to continue burning evenly. That is knocking or pinging, which sounds like a hammer striking metal. It is most likely to occur during acceleration or while climbing hills, when demands on the engine are greatest. Besides making a bothersome noise, knocking reduces power and, especially when sustained at high speeds, can cause severe engine damage.

There are two ways to reduce or eliminate knocking. One is to have a mechanic retard the spark, changing the engine timing so that the air-gas mixture is ignited a split second later in the cycle. This reduces the pressure build-up from combustion so there is less tendency for the unburned portion of fuel to detonate. It might allow the safe use of gasoline that previously made the engine knock. But it also will reduce power, giving the car less acceleration.

The second method is to use a fuel with a higher octane. At most gasoline stations, that means going from regular-grade to premium-grade gas and paying an additional four or five cents a gallon. An economy-minded driver might first try another brand of regular; it just might be better suited for his car, even if it happens to have the same octane rating. Or he can visit a station with intermediate blends of gasoline. Sunoco is the leader in this field in the Midwest, East, and South. Sears, Roebuck & Co. also operates stations with blending pumps. Some stations, including Gulf and Esso, offer three grades of gasoline.

There are three common methods of determining octane ratings. Each yields a different result. Research octane numbers are the least reliable in predicting performance. Research octane is measured by comparing a sample in a single-speed, one-cylinder laboratory test engine with that of a standard reference fuel of known octane. The comparison loses some validity when the gasoline then is used in a multi-cylinder automobile engine on the road.

A somewhat better test yields the motor octane number. The test is similar, but the laboratory engine is adjusted to simulate more rigorous operating conditions. The motor octane number of a fuel usually is several points lower than the research number. Regular gasolines today average 94.2 in research octane and 86.2 in motor octane; premium averages 100.1 and 92.1, respectively.

The third method compares the performance of gasoline samples and reference fuels in automobiles or in sophisticated laboratory equipment that considers the effect of varying speeds, loads, and other driving conditions. The result is a road octane number that comes closest to describing what a gasoline is likely to do in a motorist's own car. These tests are quite expensive to run, however, and are less suitable than the others for frequent monitoring of gasolines on the market.

In the absence of road octane ratings, the petroleum industry often uses the average of the research and motor numbers to compare antiknock qualities, a better procedure than sole reliance on either one.

Posting even reliable octane ratings still would tend to overstate their importance. It could help a driver determine what minimum available fuel he needed to stop engine knocking at a particular moment, but he would find his requirements changing with such factors as weather, location, and cleanliness of his engine.

The same engine may require three fewer research-octane numbers when the relative humidity goes up from 20 per cent to 90 per cent in the summer. An increase in altitude from sea level to 3,000 feet may allow a drop of about five numbers. But octane requirements go up as deposits accumulate in an engine's combustion chambers or if a thermostat is changed, raising an engine's operating temperature.

At present, oil companies compensate for many variables by adjusting their gasolines to the localities in which they are used. High-altitude cities, such as Denver, get lower-octane fuel than New York City. The Central Plains states, with fewer hills to exert heavy demands on engines, also are given lower-octane gasolines. And fuels are adjusted for humidity and temperature, including seasonal changes, in most parts of the country.

"Judging a gasoline by its octane is like judging a woman by her height," says one engineer. Stability, sulfur content, and volatility are qualities of gasoline that are as important as octane rating, he says. These qualities seldom go below standards that would impair a particular brand's performance in most engines.

Premium gas may have some additives that regular gas does not, however. For the extra cost, a motorist may get not only higher octane, but a detergent to clean his engine and a de-icer to prevent moisture in the gas line from freezing in the winter. But there is no easy way to find out which of these additives he is getting; a station attendant may be unable to tell him.

A motorist may find that with a particular gasoline he has difficulty starting his car in cold weather, or that he suffers from vapor lock in hot weather when gasoline sometimes vaporizes in the fuel system and shuts off the flow of liquid fuel to the engine. Or he may find that he must change his spark plugs more often with one gasoline than another. These difficulties are hard to predict, and all are unrelated to octane ratings.

How Gasoline Is Rated

There is no better test device for gasoline than a person's own car, and no better test for the minimum gasoline requirement than day-to-day experience. He can serve his interests best by trial-and-error shopping for the lowest-priced gasoline that operates his car well, or by trying to have his engine adjusted for the gasoline he prefers.

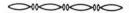

AUTOMOBILE INSURANCE COSTS continue to soar. But if you are one of the millions of motorists with $50-deductible collision insurance, you can make a significant saving on your annual premium by increasing the amount of the deductible to $100 or even $250.

Insurance rates vary greatly with geographic area, type and use of car, drivers' ages and driving records, and the insurance company itself. But a $250 deductible may halve a collision-insurance premium.

Collision insurance protects a policy owner against part or all of the cost of repairing collision damage to his own car. The owner of a deductible policy agrees to be responsible for the cost of repairs up to the amount of the deductible; anything above that is the insurance company's responsibility.

So the larger the deductible, the more you may have to pay out of your own pocket if your car is damaged. A good rule of thumb is to figure how much you could afford to pay on short notice for unanticipated repairs and make that the approximate amount of your deductible.

CAR DEALERS must post in their showrooms certain safety information about the cars they sell. Department of Transportation regulations require display of the results of manufacturers' tests of stopping distances, acceleration and passing capabilities, and the reserve-load capacity of various sizes of tires when used on a given model.

Muffler Problems

AUTOMOBILE mufflers tend to wear out frequently and can be a real nuisance. Although there isn't very much a driver can do to prolong muffler life, there are ways to cut costs on a car that is owned by the same person for several years.

Mufflers contain compartments and baffles to cut down the noise from exhaust gases. They become noisy when internal parts fail and can be dangerous as well when the outer shell becomes damaged. Exhaust fumes containing poisonous carbon monoxide may enter the passenger compartment from underneath the car.

By far the leading cause of muffler and exhaust-pipe failure is corrosion by acids that condense from the exhaust itself. As a result, a muffler tends to corrode from the inside out. Although a muffler several months old looks intact from the outside, acids on the inside may be on the verge of eating through to the surface.

The types and amounts of corrosive acids vary with the gasoline being burned, but not enough to affect muffler corrosion significantly. What does matter is how much of the acid condenses inside the muffler and the rest of the exhaust system.

Condensation—moisture changing from a vapor to a liquid—takes place when the hot exhaust cools. So the hotter the muffler, the less the condensation. Generally, a muffler above 200 degrees Fahrenheit will not collect condensation; the acids will travel through it and be expelled as gases. Usually the exhaust system parts nearest to the engine run hottest and those near the rear of the car are coolest. So corrosion is the worst at the rear.

The most damaging moments for an exhaust system are right after the automobile engine is started, but before the muffler and exhaust pipes are heated to the boiling point. If the car is stopped before the exhaust system heats up, as on a short trip to work or the store, condensation will collect and begin its attack on the metal components.

Muffler problems multiplied when auto manufacturers began producing high-performance, eight-cylinder engines with dual exhaust systems. This means the entire system tends to operate at cooler temperatures, producing more condensation.

A poorly designed muffler or exhaust system can have cool spots that take a long time to warm up, increasing the corrosion problem. And road spray containing de-icing salts will foster corrosion on the outside of the muffler and exhaust pipes. However, this exterior corrosion, even in the worst of winters, is a minor factor in exhaust-system failure.

A muffler's susceptibility to corrosion can be reduced substantially by manufacturers. A zinc or aluminum coating, now common on mufflers of even moderate cost, helps to protect the steel underneath in proportion to the coating thickness. From 1961 to 1967 the American Motors Corp. put ceramic-coated mufflers and tailpipes on its cars, guaranteeing them against corrosion as long as the original owner had the car.

Sears, Roebuck & Co. sold a ceramic-coated replacement muffler in the early 1960s, then switched for a short time to stainless steel, a nickel-chromium-iron alloy that is nearly impervious to corrosion from exhaust acids. Both of these top models carried five-year guarantees that could be transferred from one owner to the next.

But the ceramic and stainless mufflers cost quite a bit more than coated-steel mufflers and demand was small. So American Motors now puts on less-expensive aluminized mufflers carrying no guarantee. Sears' best muffler now is zinc-coated and is guaranteed for as long as the buyer owns the car on which it is installed.

Stainless-steel mufflers still are available as optional, extra-cost equipment on some higher-priced cars. Their cost is about twice that for coated-steel mufflers and could run as high as $50, not including installation. But they should last until the car heads for the junk yard.

A car owner who wants to reduce muffler maintenance headaches, but who is unable or unwilling to buy a stainless muffler, should shop for the best guarantee. Midas Muffler Shops guarantee replacement to the original buyer for a service charge of about $4. A company spokesman says Midas mufflers are made of plain steel and last an average of 30 months.

Sears and Montgomery Ward & Co. guarantee to replace their zinc-coated mufflers for nothing if the buyer still owns the car on which the muffler was installed and if installation was by a store mechanic. Their prices, with installation, usually are about the same or a little less than Midas prices.

In replacing a muffler, it is important to use one made for the particular car model involved. The wrong muffler may produce too much back pressure on the engine, thereby increasing fuel consumption, decreasing power, and possibly causing engine damage.

Coolant Equals Antifreeze

AUTOMOBILE antifreezes have changed. So have the rules of thumb for using them and the recommendations for maintaining newer cars' more dangerous cooling systems.

The major antifreeze makers have blended antileak substances into their old mixtures. They also have renamed their products, adding "summer coolant" to the titles.

The labels reflect manufacturers' desire to revise consumer thinking about the product, which today has an expanded role in car maintenance. Besides sealing small leaks and keeping ice from forming in the radiator and the engine block, modern antifreeze mixtures lubricate the water pump, inhibit rust and corrosion, and, in summer, cool the engine better than water alone possibly can. Indeed, antifreeze is as important in summer as it is in winter.

Burly, modern car engines generate tremendous heat. Combustion temperatures can reach 4,500 degrees. Temperatures of lubricated parts like pistons climb to 412 degrees.

To keep engines operating at high but efficient temperatures car manufacturers had to keep the water in cooling systems from boiling at 212 degrees, its normal sea-level boiling point. They began using pressure caps on radiators. The caps commonly used today facilitate the buildup of from 9 to 15 pounds of pressure in the cooling system.

Since each pound of pressure raises water's boiling point about three degrees, water at 15 pounds of pressure boils at about 250 degrees. That is sufficient for most engines but it doesn't provide much of a safety margin, particularly in very hot weather.

In 1962 car makers first started putting an ethylene glycol-base, "permanent" antifreeze and coolant in the radiators of cars leaving the factory. Now practically all cars are so equipped.

Antifreeze-coolants made of ethylene glycol have higher boiling temperatures than water. And if put under 15 pounds of pressure, a solution of 44 per cent ethylene glycol and 56 per cent water will not boil until it reaches 264 degrees. This gives more of a margin of safety before the radiator contents turn to vapor, causing the radiator to boil over. Most dashboard radiator-temperature warning lights turn on at 250 degrees.

The switch to ethylene glycol for year-around radiator and engine protection has had a variety of consequences. For one thing, it had made it necessary for motorists to use extreme care when tinkering with the radiator cap of a normally hot engine.

Loosening the cap releases the pressure in the cooling system. The pressure release dramatically lowers the boiling point of the fluid, and in an instant the fluid, which has already passed its normal boiling temperature, turns into a geyser of superheated steam that can seriously scald anyone close to the engine.

Though car and antifreeze makers repeatedly have warned against removing radiator caps from autos that have been running, motorists and service station attendants frequently are burned while doing just that.

It is necessary to check the fluid level in the car occasionally. If the car isn't overheating, once a month is often enough. Chrysler recommends checking it once every two months. The best time to check is when the engine is cold.

All manufacturers advise caution. They suggest removing the cap in stages, turning it first to a midpoint where the cap loosens but is still anchored in place. Then, after any steam has hissed away, the cap can be turned the rest of the way and released.

Even the relatively infrequent radiator checks might not be necessary if permanent antifreeze were trully permanent. But it is not. Investigators for the Society of Automotive Engineers have concluded that it is even less permanent than most auto makers think.

Car manufacturers generally recommend keeping factory-supplied antifreeze in the automobile for two years. Tests show, however, that the solution tends to lose its cooling qualities and its rust inhibitors after about a year or after about 30,000 miles of driving.

Rust inhibitors are important, for metals in high-temperature engines do tend to rust and corrode. Relatively small amounts of rust can hamper proper functioning of the cooling system and ultimately force engine overheating.

The safe rule for guarding against this is to empty, flush, and refill the cooling system each year. It is best to have a mechanic do the job. The traditional, handyman method of draining the radiator by opening the radiator drain, dunking a garden hose into the radiator neck, and squirting fresh water through the pipes and tubes can leave as much as half of the old solution in the far reaches of the system.

Improving on the traditional garden-hose method by using radiator-cleaner chemicals may not adequately purify the system either. Yet the system should be thoroughly cleaned because remaining, worn antifreeze will cause the needed fresh antifreeze to deteriorate considerably faster than it ordinarily would.

"Back flushing" will completely purge the system. Prestone sells a do-it-yourself "Flushing Kit" for about $3. The kit isn't hard to use. But it involves eight distinct steps, including cutting a heater hose and inserting a device that permits coupling a garden hose to the heater hose, through which back flushing can be accomplished.

The amount of antifreeze needed is calculated differently now than it used to be. Instead of putting in just enough to match expected low temperatures in the area, technicians advise keeping a half water, half antifreeze solution in the radiator all year.

The half-and-half mixture will protect against freezing to about minus 34 degrees, and at the same time provide maximum cooling efficiency in summer. In some areas more antifreeze may be needed. But motorists should avoid the extremes of entirely filling the radiator with antifreeze or of letting the antifreeze content slip below one-third.

MOTORING GUIDES: European road maps for several countries, similar in design to U.S. road maps, are available for 25 cents each from Esso European Travel Aids, P.O. Box 802, Poughkeepsie, N.Y. 12602. Add 25 cents for mailing and another 25 cents if you want special handling for delivery sooner than 10 days to two weeks. Checks and money orders should be made payable to "European Maps." Those available are for Austria, Belgium, Denmark, Finland, France, Germany, Great Britain and Ireland, Greece, Italy, Netherlands, Norway, Spain and Portugal, Sweden, and Switzerland.

Group Auto Insurance

GROUP life and health insurance policies have been available for a long time, but only recently has group auto insurance become available through employers.

Under a group plan, an insurance company sells collision and liability insurance to the employes of a firm. Except in a few states, the insurance company is allowed to exclude any employe it considers a poor risk, although this right is seldom exercised.

Each employe who participates in a group auto plan determines the extent of coverage desired and pays rates tailored to the coverage. The employer makes no contribution, but simply takes on the administrative expense of withholding each employe's premium from his pay. These payroll deductions are periodically sent to the insurance company in a single check.

This technique reduces an insurance company's overhead and enables a smaller team of agents to bring in more customers. Thus the insurance company can usually afford to offer a discount. An insurance subsidiary of CNA Financial Corp. of Chicago estimates its policyholders will normally save up to 15 per cent on their premiums by going through their employer to get group insurance. CNA lets an employe assume an individual policy at the group rate if he leaves the employ of a company participating in a group plan.

An employe may reap no benefit at all from group auto insurance if he lives in an area where state regulations already keep insurance rates low. In such areas, an insurance company may give little or no group reduction, and the employe will do well to shop around, particularly among the large insurance companies, for the most advantageous premium.

Group auto coverage is primarily available from companies such as CNA and Travelers Corp., which are heavily involved in commercial insurance. These companies use their business connections to help them set up group auto insurance for employes within a plant.

If a car owner can't get group auto insurance where he works, he may be able to get it through an association or club. This would rule out the convenience of payroll deductions, and the policyholder would be billed at home. Another possibility is to join with friends and neighbors in a co-operative. However, most states require that citizens have a reason for associating other than to seek group coverage before they can buy group insurance through a co-operative.

The high-risk driver who is likely to be turned down or charged hefty rates by an insurance company should count himself lucky if he can get coverage under a "true-group" plan. Under this type of insurance, now in very limited use, the rates for all participating employes in a company are set according to characteristics of the whole group. High-risk and low-risk drivers are charged the same basic premiums and the employer may pay part of the cost.

Cutting Auto Insurance Costs

AUTOMOBILE insurance continues to grow more expensive. But some cost-reducing options remain open to the car owner. Here are some factors he can control to reduce the cost of his premium:

✔ Driver training. This will cut a liability premium significantly for persons under 21, especially for an unmarried male under 18. Under the plan of the Insurance Rating Board (IRB) in New York City, which is representative of most insurance plans, such young car owners are automatically regarded as high-risk drivers and are charged a stiff extra premium which can be reduced by completion of a driver-training course.

✔ Engine power. Anyone who buys certain "muscle" or high-performance cars will pay about 15 per cent more for insurance coverage other than liability. Under the IRB plan, pre-1970 cars will be considered high-performance vehicles if the ratio of weight to horsepower is 10-to-1 or less. The 1970 and subsequent models get the extra-premium classification if they have a weight-to-horsepower ratio of 10.5-to-1 or less. Some non-IRB members charge more. Nationwide Mutual Insurance Co. of Columbus, Ohio, adds 50 per cent to physical-damage and liability premiums if a car with automatic transmission has a weight-to-horsepower ratio of 10.9-to-1 or less, or 11.9-to-1 or less and manual shift.

✔ Commuting distance. The cost of insurance on a car used in going to and from work increases with the distance involved. Though the savings may be relatively modest, the budget conscious may wish to consider this factor if options exist as to residence location or use of commuter buses and trains. Under the IRB rates, most men who drive more than six miles to and from work must pay a 13 per cent surcharge. The extra premium is 29 per cent if the round trip totals more than 20 miles.

✔ Use for pleasure or business. The two-car family usually will do better to designate one of its cars as exclusively for non-business use. A surcharge on liability insurance is added if a car is used in the course of commuting or performing duties on the job. Under the IRB plan, a middle-aged salesman who uses his own car for business will pay a 31 per cent surcharge.

✔ School record. A student who studies hard can cut the cost of his liability insurance. The benefit will be especially valuable for the student who would otherwise be high-risk. Under the IRB plan, a 17-year-old, unmarried boy who hasn't had driver training and uses his car for pleasure will get a 23 per cent discount if he qualifies in the judgment of his insurance company as a good student.

✔ Value of the car. Anyone in the market for a car should remember that the more expensive the car, the higher his collision-damage premium will be. A New York City resident could pay $1,136 annually for modest liability and collision coverage of a Cadillac, but the cost would drop to $767 for a Mustang.

✔ Number of cars in family. The driver who owns more than one car will benefit by insuring them with the same company. He will get a 20 per cent discount on both his liability and collision policies for each car under the IRB plan.

✔ Size of car. A compact car not only will burn less gas, but it can also make liability insurance cheaper. The current IRB plan makes no provision for compact cars, but an older plan in some states gives a 10 per cent discount. Allstate Insurance Co. of Northbrook, Ill., gives 20 per cent off on physical-damage and liability premiums.

🗸 Body design. The person who buys a car with strong bumpers, if the auto industry ever gets back to providing them, may pay less for collision insurance soon. Allstate has plans to give a 20 per cent discount on cars whose front and rear bumpers can be shown to hold up under crash tests at five m.p.h.

Other factors may reduce premiums but cannot always be controlled by the car owner. The careful driver who can avoid traffic violations and accidents will get a lower liability premium. The maximum surcharge for a bad record can more than double a premium under the IRB plan.

Anyone who lives in a large city will be more likely to have a higher liability and collision premium than a resident of a less populated area. Auto-insurance companies say the risk of accidents and vandalism is high in urban areas. The Cadillac owner in New York City will pay some $700 more for insurance than he would pay in, say, Urbana, Ohio, a town of about 11,000.

YOUR AUTO LIABILITY insurance may meet the minimums required in your state but does it meet the minimums of other states and countries? If not, you may have to post a cash bond or arrange for some other form of security if you are involved in an accident. Most states require at least $10,000 in insurance for bodily injury to any one person plus $20,000 for bodily injuries to all persons in an accident plus $5,000 for property damage. Some states, however, require much more. Check with your insurance agent for a policy endorsement or special policy to cover requirements in Canadian provinces and in Mexico.

Car Leasing

LEASING automobiles has become a popular alternative for individuals who want new cars every two or three years but want to avoid some of the bother of owning them. They can save the time and trouble involved in shopping for a car and also consolidate several costs into one uniform monthly payment to a leasing firm.

The total cost of leasing a car usually is more than for outright purchase. But the added costs sometimes can be offset at least partially. Some persons can qualify to deduct lease payments as business expenses on Federal income-tax returns. Also, the capital that would be tied up in automobile ownership can be used as an investment to earn money.

As an example, compare the two-year costs of leasing and buying a four-door hardtop, with automatic transmission, power brakes and steering, and air conditioning. A leasing firm in the Washington, D.C., area offers this car for $137 a month under a two-year lease which includes sales tax and registration fees for the car. Not included are gasoline, oil, maintenance, or insurance. After two years the lessee would have paid $3,288 but the car would still belong to the leasing firm.

One could buy the same car in the Washington area for about $4,000. Assume he traded in a used car for a $1,500 credit and borrowed the remaining $2,500 from a bank to be repaid in two years at about $115 per month. Interest on the loan would total about $260. He also would pay $160 in sales tax and about $65 for registration for two years. His total cost for obtaining the car would be $4,485, but at the end of two years he would own a vehicle worth an estimated $1,625. That leaves a net cost of $2,860, or $428 less than under the lease.

Someone who uses a car exclusively for business purposes, such as a traveling salesman, can deduct all of his automobile expenses on his income-tax return. So if he leases the four-door hardtop, he could deduct an additional $428 over a two-year period. If this person's annual income were $20,000 and he filed a joint return, the increased deduction would save him about $120 in taxes, reducing the extra cost of leasing to $308.

The extra net cost of leasing could be reduced further if the lessee sells the old car he would have traded in on a new car and invests the sale proceeds. If he gets $1,500 for the old car and makes an investment yielding 10 per cent a year, he would have earned about $250 in two years after taxes. If this investment gain ($250) plus the tax savings ($120) are deducted from the $428 extra cost of leasing the hardtop in the example above, the net additional lease cost is reduced to $58.

Keep in mind, however, that any such closing of the lease-cost gap is available primarily to persons eligible to deduct transportation costs from tax returns as a business expense. Taxes, indeed, might even go up for a person who leases a vehicle for family-and-pleasure use. Here's why: The interest on money borrowed to *buy* a car is always deductible from tax returns; no part of what is paid to *lease* a car to be used for nonbusiness purposes may be deducted. So leasing could add $30 to $40 a year to a tax bill.

The convenience and the cost of leasing automobiles varies considerably with the coverage of the lease, the length of its term, and the type of car leased. The most expensive leases have full maintenance and insurance coverage. Most are for two years, but usually they can be extended at an over-all reduction in annual cost.

Although leasing firms often advertise that they will lease any car a customer wants, generally they don't handle foreign cars and some of the more specialized American models that depreciate rapidly. Some firms prefer to deal with cars from a particular manufacturer, often because they are affiliated with that corporation and can obtain the cars at lower cost.

Generally, the more a car costs to buy and operate, the more it costs to lease; a Chevrolet can be leased for about $75 a month, while a Cadillac goes for more than $180. These prices are for the simplest type of agreement, the finance lease. It covers just the cost of obtaining a new car, with the lessee driving it as if he had bought it. He arranges and pays for registration, maintenance, gasoline, insurance, and any local taxes assessed on the car. His monthly lease payments are like those he would make to a bank or other credit agency had he borrowed money to buy the car. The chief advantage is that, except for a possible security deposit, the lease requires no trade-in or down payment as a purchase does.

Leases may be of the open-end or closed-end type. In an open-end lease, the customer agrees to take some financial responsibility by, in effect, guaranteeing that the leasing firm will get the depreciated wholesale value of the car at the end of the term.

This value is estimated at the beginning of the lease period after looking at average depreciation of similar cars over the previous months or years. When the lease expires, the lessee buys the car for this predetermined wholesale price. He is then free to sell the car.

If he gets more than the estimate, his net leasing cost is reduced; if it sells for less, his cost is increased.

There is a danger in an open-end lease. The leasing firm may overestimate the depreciated value of a car to make the lease more attractive: The higher the estimate, the lower the payments. But the lessee will be stuck with a costlier obligation at the end of the lease.

Because the lessee is assuming some financial risk, the monthly payments under an open-end lease usually are lower than under the closed-end type, where his only obligation is to return the automobile in reasonable condition. Then the leasing company bears the risk itself of getting back a less valuable car than it had planned on.

A customer can help his cause by leasing a car that is expected to hold its value reasonably well over the leasing period—advice that is valid in buying a car as well. Such a car today might have an automatic transmission, air conditioning, power brakes and steering, a radio, and, unless it is a compact model, an eight-cylinder engine.

Leases are not always easy to compare. Some firms pay for the car's registration and local sales or road taxes, charging slightly higher monthly rates as a result. Some give the customer several choices at the end of the lease period, such as extending the lease at a lower rate, selling the car and paying the predetermined wholesale value, or merely returning the car. These leases contain the features of both open-end and closed-end leases.

Insurance coverage usually adds $15 to $25 to monthly lease payments. A full-maintenance lease can cost an extra $20 or so a month, but the customer may gain such conveniences as having snow tires installed for the winter and getting a replacement car while the regular car is being serviced. Another benefit comes in budgeting automobile expenses, because maintenance costs will never exceed the known monthly figure, no matter what must be done to the car. Full-maintenance leases, however, may cease to cover repairs after a maximum mileage. Some leasing firms discourage maintenance options, contending that most major, unexpected costs are covered by new-car warranties.

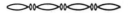

TIRE ROTATION is even more important with new tires designed to give extra-long mileage, the Firestone Tire & Rubber Co. warns. Tires should be rotated every 5,000 miles so that wear on each will be as even as possible. Front tires tend to wear first on their outer edges because of steering action. Rear tires tend to wear more heavily in the center through transmitting thrust to the road.

NEW-CAR SHOPPERS may wish to determine whether a dealer will correct minor deficiencies found in a new car without requiring the owner to leave the vehicle in the dealer's repair shop all day. Dealers have been known to insist that new-car owners give up their cars for a day for such five-minute jobs as replacing a cracked battery or even for installing lugs that the manufacturer failed to put on a wheel.

AUTOMOTIVE HEAD RESTRAINTS are rarely adjusted to give maximum protection in an accident, says the National Safety Council. The cushions should be adjusted so that their tops are no lower than the tops of the drivers' or passengers' ears. In a horizontal plane, the restraints should be from 1 to 6 inches behind the seat occupant's head.

Diagnosing Car Troubles

ELECTRONIC diagnostic centers may help a car owner determine what shape his car is in. There are now several hundred such facilities in the country, ranging from one-car slots in service stations to long lanes in special buildings that can handle a dozen cars at once in assembly-line fashion. The expensive, sophisticated equipment used in the larger of these centers probably offers the best means now available to discover defective, worn-out, and maladjusted items on a car, but the owner still should be wary of the test results.

A complete diagnostic center includes this equipment:

✔ A dynamometer, a set of rollers in the floor that allows a car's wheels to spin so the engine can be tested in simulated driving conditions.

✔ A dynamic brake tester, which also simulates road travel with rollers, often an integral part of the dynamometer.

✔ Front-end alignment and wheel balance testing devices, which together test front-end stability.

✔ An oscilloscope and related gear to test electronically whether the engine is running properly.

✔ A chassis lift to simplify under-car inspection.

With this equipment and with a thorough visual inspection of the car, trained diagnosticians can check the performance of an amazing number of items, sometimes as many as 500, including the clutch, water pump, transmission, and steering mechanisms. The process takes about an hour at most centers and may cost from $6 to $24. Tests like these are considerably more complete than the typical state inspections, which cover primarily safety items.

Drivers have a variety of reasons for wanting their cars diagnosed. They bring in used cars they are considering buying, cars they want tested before warranties expire, cars they intend to take on long vacation trips, cars in need of some undetermined repair, and cars they are thinking of trading in on new ones.

Choosing a center can be a trial. Those independent of any repair facility are generally considered the most reliable because they lack a selfish interest in finding defects. But they are scarce, they tend to be more expensive, and trips to other facilities will be needed for even simple repairs. When making price comparisons, consider the thoroughness of the diagnosis and the completeness of the equipment used. A center without a dynamometer, for example, cannot check the engine under highway stress. If possible, ask other motorists for their experiences with local centers.

An experiment in the Washington, D.C., area shows the surprises a car owner can find in having his car examined for the first time. Two centers were chosen from the telephone yellow pages. Both promised electronic testing, required appointments, and seemed similar in other ways, including price.

At the first, run by a large auto-repair company, the car owner sat in a plush, high-backed chair in a paneled room, listened to piped-in FM music, and watched through a plate-glass window as his car traveled through the test lane. As each of 150 tests was completed, the diagnostician in a white coverall punched a button on an electronic clipboard, activating a print-out device in front of the owner that showed the results.

The procedure was fascinating and efficient. No major deficiencies were found, but six minor failures were reported: a leaking valve-cover gasket, a corroded battery cable, dirty air filters, a worn heater hose, a worn generator belt, and poor windshield wiper blades. These, plus a few optional adjustment items, were explained in layman's language by the center's manager after the testing. There was no pressure to have any repairs made there, although free estimates and a free reinspection were offered as incentives. The testing cost $12.

The second test location was a dirty repair bay in a small service station. Half the portable electronic gear was out of order. As the owner stood next to his car, the diagnostician poked around under the hood and made such reports as, "That generator belt needs replacing real bad." An oscilloscope pattern puzzled the attendant until he studied a manual and asked the station manager for help. Then he said the engine was running a little roughly and suggested that either the coil or condenser needed replacement. Both had passed with flying colors at the first center.

He followed no check list and wrote nothing down during the test, but he did discover the poor wiper blades, the corroded battery cable, and the leaking gasket. He said nothing about the heater hose and air cleaners and glanced only quickly under the car. As an afterthought, he asked the owner to turn on the various lights so he could check them.

This second diagnosis seemed superficial, haphazard, and hardly worth the 45 minutes it took. The charge, normally $13, was reduced to $5 because of the faulty equipment. Even a complete test would have been less complete than the one at the first center, however, for there was no dynamometer, dynamic brake test equipment, and front-end test equipment in the service station.

A motorist having his car diagnosed should remember that even fancy equipment properly maintained requires subjective interpretation of results. Some mechanics may want to replace slightly worn items unnecessarily, and the owner should try to determine which repairs are absolutely required and which are optional. Remember that a used car need not perform like a new one to provide good service. Finally, if repairs are made, a recheck of those items is advisable; many centers do this for a minimal extra fee, if any.

A DAYDREAMING MOTORIST can be detected by a new automobile accessory and audibly warned to pay more attention to the road, says the manufacturer, Life Technology, Inc., 2346 Stanwell Drive, Concord, Calif. 94520. The device utilizes research indicating that every person has his own rate of making small steering adjustments while driving. The new accessory, named LTI-OWL, measures this "wheel-reversal rate" for a few minutes each time a car is driven and stores the pattern in a small memory bank. If the driver's reversal rate drops, a beeper sounds to warn him of the possibility that he is not concentrating fully on driving or that he is tired. If the rate becomes abnormally high, an amber light comes on to suggest that the car may be going too fast for safety. The device costs $314 plus installation and is the approximate size of an automobile radio.

ALL TIRES, including private or off brands, must bear a manufacturer's code number assigned by the Department of Transportation (DOT). The number is preceded by the initials DOT. Dealers should identify the manufacturer of a tire upon request.

Grease Jobs—A Slippery Area

IN recent years U.S. auto makers have been producing cars with special, sealed steering and suspension joints, which, they say, practically eliminate the need for grease jobs. And for as long as Detroit has been using the seals, garage mechanics have been advising car owners to equip them with old-fashioned fittings that permit greasing with a pressurized grease "gun" at regular intervals.

The mechanics argue that the new, sealed systems, which allegedly block out contaminants, do not provide optimum lubrication for as long as Detroit says they do. The mechanics say that to get long life and top performance from a car it should be greased every 2,000 or 3,000 miles.

The fittings cost from 20 to 50 cents each. The total cost of installing fittings runs from about $5 to $8. That's a small price for the assurance that you always have clean, high-viscosity lubricant protecting parts, some mechanics contend.

Yet service managers at new-car dealerships normally resist tampering with the sealed-in grease systems until the manual says to. For most cars that's at 36,000 miles or at 36 months, whichever comes first.

If the car owner has the neighborhood mechanic install grease-gun fittings on sealed joints, the owner may void his car warranty. Even if he has the dealer's service center do it, he may invalidate his warranty unless he returns the car to the dealership for greasing at frequent, stipulated times. This often is more bother than the car owner wants.

One solution to the grease or not-to-grease dilemma.

Leave the car's sealed-in grease system intact. If the car begins riding roughly, have the dealer's service department examine the suspension system for such things as damaged springs or shock absorbers or for improperly adjusted shock absorbers. These may be causing the hard ride. If not, insist on a thorough check of sealed joints.

The matter of greasing is important, and not just because it makes a car ride better. Unlubricated or improperly lubricated parts quickly chip, crack, or grind apart under normal driving stresses. Some of the parts involved are crucial; they control steering and other vital functions.

In the past, motorists tended to neglect periodic greasing of cars with grease-gun fittings. Car makers knew this. They realized that as they turned out faster and more powerful automobiles, lack of regular lubrication might create serious safety problems. Consequently they took advantage of the advent of longer-lasting greases and tougher joints and bearings to put together the sealed systems.

Some independent automotive engineers say the sealed systems do give average motorists the best protection against premature breakdowns. Greases the manufacturers install generally are better than those stocked by service stations. Also, manufacturers force grease into the systems with hand-powered grease guns, whereas service stations commonly use power tools that ram the lubricant into the car under pressure so high it can damage the joint.

Buying a Used Car

"THE transmission leaks. It's worn out. I'll tell you though, I'm not replacing it. This car's too sick to bother with any more." With that our neighborhood mechanic sent my wife and me scurrying after our sixth car—our sixth *used* car.

We knew the truth of the adage: Buy a used car and you buy another man's troubles. Too-frequent, routine repairs to our last two cars had cost $1,061.30. But we are among those who just don't desire or can't afford high payments for new cars. We thought that this time if we studied and shopped carefully, we could find a sound, reasonably priced used vehicle.

We found right off that much how-to-buy-a-used-car advice in magazines isn't particularly practical. And we discovered again that used-car buying is an endless series of compromises; that the chance of being gypped is high.

Then we located state car-inspection officials and a candid used-car salesman. They gave us clues to our errors in buying our sixth car plus the counsel we should have had at the outset.

In the past we had relied on friends in the business to help us buy. We purchased our last two automobiles from the friend of a clergyman. The cars looked to be in fine shape, like "low-mileage cream puffs," as they were described. They cost just what we could afford. But both cars leaked like battered buckets. One had an insatiable appetite for oil and an eerie electrical system; its tail lights would turn themselves on to burn all night if not noticed.

This time we would go about things differently; we would be systematic. We calculated how much we could spend without financing—about $1,600. To that was added $100 for possible repairs to get the next purchase in really good shape. We needed a nine-passenger station wagon. But because they cost more and are hard to find, we were prepared to settle for a six-passenger wagon.

Then we went to the most helpful guide that is widely available, the "frequency-of-repair" charts annually published in "The Buying Guide Issue of Consumer Reports" by Consumers Union (CU), the nonprofit, product-testing group. The charts show whether a particular model has had more- or less-than-normal trouble with piston rings, the electrical system, valves, and the like. They are a rough guide to the durability of recent automobiles.

The Buying Guide also gives used-car purchasing advice and lists retail car prices. The price lists are only general indicators because prices vary month to month from region to region.

The buying advice is logical but sometimes impossible to heed. For instance, the book details nine on-the-lot tests and eight driving tests to make before buying. But salesmen sometimes reacted sullenly when I produced a list of the tests and started zipping windows up and down, adjusting and readjusting seats, and rocking cars to see if the shock absorbers worked. (Good shock absorbers should level a car immediately after rocking is halted; if shocks are defective, the car will continue rocking up and down for several cycles.)

We visited lots too jammed to walk around and lots where the lights made it difficult to spot dents and fresh paint, the traditional indicators of body damage. We concluded night buying had to be avoided.

What's more, streets near many used-car lots were too clogged to allow stops from 45 miles per hour and other recommended driving tests.

At one lot, where we interrupted an employes' card game to look at a Dodge, the dealer became annoyed when after several other tests I asked to drive the car. "Give it a try," he said, handing me the keys. But testing was impossible; I couldn't have squeezed a bicycle through the only opening to the street. The salesman, clearly not interested in a customer who wanted a test drive, refused to move the cars blocking the driveway and galumphed back to his card game.

Nonetheless the guide helped us pinpoint nine models that fit our criteria. At a library, I checked actual car prices in the second most important buyer aid, the noncirculating copy of *The Red Book: Official Used Car Valuations*.

Many libraries have the *Red Book* or equivalent "Blue" or "Black" books. Another popular guide is the National Automobile Dealers' Association *Official Used Car Guide*. The guides give average retail and wholesale prices for all models still widely sold. The books are reliable; they are the salesman's own source of price information. But the books come in different editions for different parts of the nation. It is imperative that the buyer check the edition containing data for the geographic area where he will be buying.

While I studied the books, my wife scanned newspaper advertisements for clues to dealers with cars we might be interested in. She made a master list. Then she started phoning. Invariably salesmen said they had models we wanted. Yet when we arrived to examine the cars, we were told they had "just been sold" and we were steered to others. It was a variation on the familiar "bait-and-switch" routine.

Subsequent chats with men familiar with nearly every phase of used-car marketing indicate that we were lucky and that our shopping effort omitted several important steps. 1680464

Norman Polovoy, assistant state attorney general and chief of Maryland's consumer protection division, insists:

"A buyer should be searching and inquiring. He should find out from the dealer who the previous owner was. If the dealer won't tell, the buyer should look elsewhere. If he does tell, the buyer should get on the phone. His first question: 'What was the approximate mileage when the car was traded?' Most owners know within 5,000 miles. Secondly, he should ask: 'Has the car been in an accident?' Thirdly, he should ask why the car was traded. That fills in important missing links." In our hunt we did none of these things.

We had shopped the lots indiscriminately. This was a mistake according to Rogers Ecolono. Mr. Ecolono is a salesman for a new-car dealer in Baltimore. He has been hawking used cars for 22 years, and he knows the ropes.

He agrees with Consumers Union that it is best always to buy used cars from a franchised, new-car dealer. There is more likelihood then of getting a one-owner car traded on a new one. Most independent dealers get their vehicles from fleet owners, wholesale auctioneers, and new-car sellers.

Mr. Ecolono also suggests buying used cars between August and March when prices are lowest. He recommends shopping at a big dealership selling the most expensive cars—Cadillacs, Lincolns, and Imperials. There, he believes, used cars tend to be given true mechanical reconditioning. The dealer passes the cost to the buyer, but the buyer can expect to get a better car there even if it isn't one of the dealer's own luxury models.

We didn't know that. Nor were we aware, as Mr. Ecolono says, that light-colored cars, especially white ones, and "hot models with eye" (short for eye appeal) cost more just because they are popular. Buyers concerned with economy might avoid them. Current hot models in the East are Chevrolet Impalas, Ford Galaxie 500s, and Plymouth Sport Furies, says Mr. Ecolono.

He also asserts that even buyers who know nothing about mechanical things should check the oil in cars they look at. Dirty motor oil indicates the seller cares less than normal about reconditioning.

After four, intense days of hunting, we found the car we wanted at a used-car lot operated by a Maryland Chrysler-Plymouth dealer. It was an air-conditioned, 1967 Plymouth wagon with a staved-in tailgate and a "not very negotiable" $1,750 price tag. Of course, it was a compromise. It was a six-passenger model; it cost more than we wanted to pay; it was maroon. My wife preferred a lighter color.

But we were flexible. So we looked it over carefully. Besides the smashed rear we noted: missing instrument knobs, a wobbly rear-view mirror, a seat that wouldn't adjust, a warning light that continually signaled the emergency brake was on when it wasn't, and a broken directional-light switch.

We made a tentative decision to buy and made a $25 deposit. The salesman said our "little complaints" would be remedied and the car would be ready for pick up in three days. We asked the salesman to note on the deposit receipt that the sale was contingent on our approval of the car after inspection by our own mechanic. Every used-car buyer should do this.

Five days passed before the car finally was "all set

to go." My wife took it to our mechanic. She had trouble driving. The seat still wouldn't adjust properly, the rear-view mirror still drooped, the directional lights kept signaling a left turn, and the brake-warning light incessantly blinked. Also, there was no key for the lock on the tailgage replacement.

Our mechanic reported two more faults: a burned-out motor on the windshield cleaning-fluid pumps and a leak in the power-steering system. He told us that the car was essentially sound, however, and worth buying if the directional lights, power-steering leak, and mirror were fixed. He doubted that the dealer would do more than that.

The dealer did fix those three things and we bought the car. He said he had no key for the tailgate so we had to get a set made. We also learned to jiggle the wires on the brake signal to turn it off.

Then we made an anticipated expenditure of $103.19 for a tune up, oil change, and installation of heavy-duty shock absorbers.

At this point we wondered if the travail was worth it. As far as could be determined we had a sturdy automobile, which should give us a couple of years of relatively trouble-free service. It was clean and presentable. But the trips to the library, the phoning, the lot hopping—well, it was rather much.

According to Anthoney Till, car salesman, dealer, and author of *What You Should Know Before You Buy a Car,* (Shelbourne Press, Inc., 1640 S. La Cienega Blvd., Los Angeles 90035; 235 pages; $4.95), it is rare for dealers ever to do more than give a used car "appearance reconditioning." This includes polishing or painting plus putting heavy oil and additives in the motor and transmission.

It is also unusual for salesmen to tell customers

whether or not cars they are buying have seen debilitating duty as taxis, police, or rental cars. Chances are good that the buyer will be shown one.

"More than one of 10 used cars sold today were used by police, or cab companies, or firms like Hertz," says Mr. Ecolono.

To keep from being stuck with a late-model cab that is just miles from exhaustion, the buyer should look for holes drilled under the dashboard. They may have been put there to accommodate a two-way radio or a taxi meter. A new ceiling liner in a late-model car is a tip off. New headliners often are put in to hide patch work resulting when roof lights are removed.

A one-year-old taxicab or police car may easily have traveled more than 125,000 miles. But the odometer or mileage meter rarely will reflect this. Except in a very few states, dealers often pay itinerant odometer "artists" to set back the mileage. These specialists usually turn back the first number; they do an almost undetectable job.

In 1966, Maryland passed legislation requiring presale inspection and certification of vehicles. The inspection covers numerous safety items, including brakes, tires, exhaust system, and steering. The law is rigidly enforced.

As a result, a buyer in Maryland presumably has a better chance of getting a mechanically good car. Dealers know they must repair safety defects, so they tend to stock only machines requiring minimum repairs.

To some extent this upgrading of used-car quality has occurred in the 14 other states with presale inspections and in the District of Columbia and the 31 states that now have periodic motor vehicle checks.

Yet, according to Mr. Polovoy, Maryland's law and the others have limited effect.

"The law was intended to clear roads of the motorized debris," says Mr. Polovoy. "It helped. But we still get a tremendous number of used-car complaints—150 a week. You can still take the used-car sales situation here and trace every type of consumer fraud and deception there is."

California's consumer protection department reports only about 80 used-car complaints a week. The state has no periodic or presale motor-vehicle inspections.

Even in states with both kinds of laws, lack of enforcement can blunt their impact. Some Southern states have such laws and still are dumping grounds for auto cast-offs.

When the salesman who sold us our car told us he would allow us $200 on our trade-in, he explained that the old car was in such poor shape it would have to be resold to another dealer and "shipped down South" for retailing.

It is pretty clear that persons buying used cars in the South—anywhere—must take elaborate pains if they are to get good ones.

—AUGUST GRIBBIN

SLOW-MOVING VEHICLES now are required to display a triangular emblem in many states to warn motorists approaching from the rear that they are traveling at speeds under 25 miles per hour. The emblem, 16 inches wide and 15 inches high, combines an orange fluorescent center for high daytime visibility with a red reflective border that can be picked up by headlights at night a quarter of mile away.

Trailers and Towing Tricks

IF you are planning to join the ranks of the millions of Americans who haul boat, camping, or other trailers behind their automobiles, a little planning may save money and grief.

It is important to match the trailer to the towing vehicle. A person who plans to use his present automobile should not buy a trailer that is too large and heavy for the car's towing capabilities; a person who is determined to own a specific trailer may find it advisable to buy a car with an engine, transmission, cooling system, and other equipment designed for extra duty. Cars can be modified for safe heavy-trailer duty, but a factory-installed package is probably more effective and less expensive.

Automobile manufacturers have brochures listing their towing recommendations; they can be obtained free from many local dealers. The Customer Relations Department, American Motors Corp., 14250 Plymouth Rd., Detroit, Mich. 48232, will send out a free bulletin. Robert Honke, Recreation Vehicles Manager, Ford Division, Dearborn, Mich. 48121, will provide detailed recommendations for Ford vehicles or answer specific questions; be sure to state model and year. Both American and Ford pamphlets contain information of interest to any vehicle owner who plans to tow a trailer.

The National Safety Council says that the gross weight of the towed vehicle, including all loose supplies and equipment, should not be more than one-half the weight of the towing automobile or pickup truck. That rule of thumb does not apply, however, to heavy trailers properly designed and equipped.

A Ford-sponsored book, *Camping* (The Benjamin Co., Inc., 485 Madison Ave., New York City 10022, $4.95), makes recommendations based on horsepower. A short compact auto with less than 95 horsepower, such as a Volkswagen, should not be used to tow anything over 1,000 pounds, it says. A standard U.S. car with less than 200 horsepower can tow up to 2,000 pounds; one with more than 300 horsepower can tow up to 3,800 pounds. A pickup truck probably is necessary for anything heavier.

The Society of Automotive Engineers has developed trailer classes in setting safety and performance standards. Class I trailers, which include most trailers carrying small outboard fishing boats, weigh up to 2,000 pounds fully loaded. Class II includes those from 2,000 to 3,500 pounds, such as most inboard boat trailers and many travel trailers. Class III trailers range from 3,500 to 5,000 pounds, which includes heavy travel trailers. These classifications often are stamped on new trailers or referred to in safety recommendations.

Obtaining the proper trailer hitch is essential. For lightweight trailers of less than 500 pounds, a hitch costing from $5 to $15 that simply clamps onto the bumper may be sufficient. A frame hitch, which may be bolted to the rear bumper in addition to the automobile frame, can haul trailers weighing more than 2,000 pounds if it has more than one attachment to the frame; it costs about the same as a bumper hitch, but usually has to be installed by a mechanic.

For heavy Class II trailers and all Class III trailers, an equalizing, or weight-distributing, hitch is recommended. It has arms that reach back and, when properly adjusted, place a hefty share of the trailer tongue weight on the wheels of the trailer as well as on all four wheels of the towing vehicle. This arrangement puts less strain on the automobile's rear axle and also helps keep the car and trailer level for better driving control. An equalizing hitch can cost from $60 to more than $100, plus another $25 or so for installation.

Another important factor in safe trailing is the hitch or tongue weight—the downward force at the coupling. Too little weight can result in trailer whipping, in which the trailer sways back and forth dangerously, perhaps throwing the towing vehicle out of control. Too much tongue weight can tip the car and trailer unevenly, making steering difficult. The principle holds true for both single- and double-axle trailers.

The tongue load should be between 10 and 15 per cent of the gross trailer weight. Thus, a 2,000-pound trailer should have a tongue weight of 200 to 300 pounds. An owner probably can have his trailer weighed at a municipal scale or at a local lumber or coal yard. The tongue weight usually can be checked with a bathroom scale.

Trailer brakes, applied manually by the driver or automatically when the towing vehicle's brakes are applied, are recommended for trailers weighing more than about 1,500 pounds. Some states require brakes on trailers weighing more than 40 per cent of the towing vehicle's weight. Extension rear-view mirrors costing a few dollars are advisable, and may be required by state law, for hauling any but the narrowest of trailers. Be sure to get a safety chain and the proper size ball for your trailer's coupler.

Encyclopedias for Children

CHOOSING an encyclopedia, in most families, means thinking about the use the children will make of it. Should the family seriously consider buying a set designed for younger ages? What are the differences in encyclopedias? How does one judge which set will best serve the entire family? These are a few of the questions that may occur.

Publishers offer some 20 sets designed for youngsters. Librarians report that many adults prefer to use a good children's encyclopedia because it may be more concise and better illustrated than the adult sets. Although the adult text may be more comprehensive or complete, both children and adults may find the simpler organization and readable text of the children's sets preferable.

However, parents should be aware of the differences among the children's sets. Organization of material differs considerably; some sets include specific references in broad themes that encourage browsing and reading just for fun; others have to-the-point alphabetical entries and are intended mainly as reference tools.

Some encyclopedias cover a very specific age range, whereas others are intended for general use by both children and adults. And there is a wide range in prices, from $40 to $320. So how is a careful parent to choose?

First, consider the ages of members of the family. Most children's encyclopedias are designed for a starting age of 7 to 9 and aim for a top age between 14 and 17.

Waiting until children are in or near the third grade to buy an encyclopedia is advised by several librarians, in order that the set will be as up to date as possible when it gets the most use. One Maryland librarian commented that in her experience, children seem to have little need for or interest in organized, classified approaches to information before the third grade.

However, several book sets are intended for preschoolers and very young school children. Most, such as *Childcraft* (Field Enterprises Educational Corp., Merchandise Mart Plaza, Chicago 60606; $130.90 to $140.90; 15 volumes), collect information in each volume according to topics such as "world and space."

An exception is the new *Young Children's Encyclopedia* (Encyclopaedia Britannica, 425 N. Michigan Ave., Chicago 60611; about $60, 16 volumes). It offers an alphabetical format for ages 4 to 9. Illustrations are emphasized, the reading level is intended for the beginner, and references give very basic information in simple, storylike form and large print.

For elementary and high-school students, there are about 12 general encyclopedias on the market, and several specialized ones. However, an American Library Association (ALA) reviewing committee of 50 leading librarians in the U.S. and Canada highly recommends only six of them.

Those mainly intended for elementary school pupils (children between ages 7 and 14) are the *Britannica Junior* (Encyclopaedia Britannica; $149.90; 15 volumes); *The New Book of Knowledge* (Grolier, Inc., 575 Lexington Ave., New York City 10022; $199.50; 20 volumes); and *Our Wonderful World: An Encyclopedic An-*

thology for the Entire Family (Grolier, Inc.; $189.50; 18 volumes).

Britannica Junior is not a junior version of *Encyclopaedia Britannica,* despite the similar title. Its organization and content is completely different, and it is based upon and expanded from *Weedon's Encyclopedia,* which first appeared in 1931.

Our Wonderful World is very different from the usual reference encyclopedia. It presents material not alphabetically, but grouped within five major themes such as "the Individual" and "The Physical Environment." The set, recommended by the ALA for browsing and general informational reading, was termed "a lot of fun" by one librarian.

Concentrating more on the upper elementary grades and high-school students are *Compton's Encyclopedia and Fact Index* (F. E. Compton, a subsidiary of Encyclopaedia Britannica; $184.50 to $199.50; 24 volumes); and *Merit Students Encyclopedia* (Crowell-Collier and Macmillan, Inc., 866 Third Ave., New York 10022; $319.50; 20 volumes).

Compton's is one of the sets most frequently found in public libraries and schools. Subjects are covered in broad discussions on general topics, with an excellent index and cross-reference system to guide the reader to specific items. The *Merit* encyclopedia is one of the newest sets. It was first published in 1967 and is not based on any previous set. Librarians report a good response from its users, its short specific references take a scientific tone and it is particularly useful for older children.

Among encyclopedias that can be used by children and adults, the *World Book Encyclopedia* (Field Enterprises Educational Corp.; $179.80 to $199.80; 20 volumes) is a favorite selection for children's sections in public libraries. Educators report that third graders usally are able to use it, and its wide appeal extends to adult ages.

Occasionally found in children's sections, also, is *Collier's Encyclopedia,* $329.50, a 24-volume set categorized for adult use but found to be useful for advanced children in upper elementary grades and high school as well.

Aside from those recommended by the ALA committee, there are several sets that have specific strong points. And there are lower-priced sets for between $40 and $80 that can serve a purpose where budgets are limited, although such drawbacks as brevity of coverage and oversimplification are cited by the ALA to prevent their recommendation as general reference works.

Faced with so many possibilities, parents should do some critical evaluation before deciding which set will suit their need. Some important ways to do this:

Read critical review by professionals. There is no other way to get a thorough judgment of accuracy and important technical details such as actual reading level of the writing. Detailed descriptions and evaluations of most sets are presented by the ALA committee in the "Subscription Books Bulletin." The Bulletin is available in most public libraries.

A 1969 article in the Bulletin, "Purchasing a General Encyclopedia," can be obtained for 25 cents from the ALA Publishing Services, 50 E. Huron St., Chicago, Ill. 60611. This gives detailed suggestions on what points to look for in judging encyclopedias. It also gives short ALA reviews of many sets, and lists the dates when they were reviewed in detail.

Also available in most libraries is "General Encyclopedias in Print, 1971, A Comparative Analysis," published by the R. R. Bowker Co., New York, which is an exhaustive analysis of most encyclopedias on the market with reviews that can be found in other sources listed for each set.

After reading the reviews, narrow the choice to a few preferred sets, and then compare them. There is no substitute for reading them side by side. One encyclopedia's treatment of a subject may seem excellent—until it is seen next to a different treatment which could seem still more attractive and useful.

Read articles in each of the sets on: (1) subjects familiar to you, to judge their accuracy; (2) subjects unfamiliar to you, to see how understandable they become; and (3) several controversial subjects, to judge objectivity.

Remember that illustrations are important to children. There should be an adequate number, and they should be relevant to the material being discussed.

Be sure that the index and cross-referencing is accurate and easy to use. If these are confusing, the encyclopedia loses much usefulness.

Be aware of the reference and updating services offered by the publisher of each set. Most good encyclopedias offer year-books that bring information up to date, but these vary considerably in usefulness and price.

And keep in mind the individuals who will be using an encyclopedia. Are they the quick-answer types who would prefer a concise, specific reference, or the imaginative ones who would prefer broad articles including a lot of related ideas together?

HOMEWORK again occupies many youngsters and proper lighting often can make study easier. A free Government bulletin, "Planning Your Home Lighting" contains tips on portable and permanent lighting. It is available from the Office of Information, Department of Agriculture, Washington, D.C. 20250.

Atlases—A World of Difference

B UYING a home atlas involves a complicated choice. There are, for example, more than 30,000 atlases on Library of Congress shelves. Some are relics, but many are available in bookstores. English versions range in price from less than $1, for a paperback, to more than $75. They vary in subject matter, format, and accuracy.

Two atlases, each expensive, are generally considered to be the best general-purpose volumes available in English.

One is *The Times Atlas of the World* (Times Newspapers, Ltd., London, in collaboration with John Bartholomew & Son, Ltd., Edinburgh; 272 pages; $45). This 12-pound volume led the field for many years, and some librarians specializing in cartography still rate it far and away the best written in English. Its ample index includes about 200,000 place names. The index locates cities and other geographic points by latitude and longitude rather than by a less precise key system. A separate plastic panel, explaining map abbreviations and symbols, is tucked inside to enable a user to conveniently place it beside any map.

The other atlas praised highly is Rand McNally's *International Atlas* (Rand McNally & Co., Box 7600, Chicago 60680; 547 pages, $34.95).

The *International Atlas* has an excellent system of map scales. Continents are displayed on one scale, nations on a larger scale, and cities on the largest. The effect, on turning the pages, is like bringing a magnifying glass up and down against a globe. Although this system does slight less populated places by focusing on large cities, it more than makes up for that disadvantage by lending the atlas a rare orderliness.

Inevitably, the *International Atlas* gives a bit more attention to the United States than does the *Times Atlas*. But the *International Atlas* shows more restraint than many atlases by American publishers. The only real incidence of partiality occurs in the selection of cities for individual maps: Over one-fifth of the 62 are in the United States.

About 160,000 place names are indexed in the *International Atlas,* also by latitude and longitude.

An atlas shopper may find other publications better suited to his particular needs. Historical atlases, for example, are designed to show changes in the political alignments of countries. *Goode's World Atlas* (Rand McNally & Co.; 315 pages; $7.95) is full of thematic maps on such topics as soil types, industrial development, and the occurrence of killing frosts in the United States.

Rand McNally & Co. rents an unusual book, *Commercial Atlas & Marketing Guide,* for $75 a year. It contains detailed information about tiny American towns such as the name of the railroad that runs through Danby, Calif., population 5.

Whatever the subject matter, an atlas ought to measure up to certain standards:

Maps should be attractive and clear. Garish colors may make a user bleary eyed, while somber colors often obscure place names. To avoid confusion, cities should appear in one style of print, small towns in another. Place names need to be arranged without excess overlapping.

A good index is a necessity. Some include extras such as population figures beside each entry, but the basic requirement for an index is comprehensiveness: The more place names the better. It's desirable, too, that locations of map features be indicated by latitude and longitude.

To determine whether an atlas is up to date, look up towns or countries that have recently changed names or political status. For example, Tanganyika and Zanzibar merged and became Tanzania in 1964.

Some atlases devote more space to some countries than others.

The size of an atlas is important. Small atlases often contain maps that lack detail or are so over-crowded they're impossible to read. Small atlases also are often short on text.

However, some large atlases are stuffed with color photographs and blurbs on such subjects as the flags and customs of foreign countries. A shopper may prefer to get this type of information from an almanac or an encyclopedia.

Many publishers put out catalogs that may be helpful in selecting an atlas. For a free list of atlas publishers around the world, write the Library of Congress, Geography and Map Division, Washington, D.C. 20540.

A CHALKBOARD of almost any size can be created in a child's room with a special green paint marketed by Sapolin Paints, Inc., 201 E. 42nd St., New York City 10017. The paint, "Rite-On Green," can be applied directly to a wall. Youngsters can then write or draw on the wall with chalk and erase with a chalkboard eraser or damp cloth.

Speed Reading

SPEED-READING courses still are in vogue. But a decade after the courses became popular, the curious still find it hard to get a simple answer when they ask if the regimens work.

The academics, who mainly teach traditional reading methods and devise grade-school courses and remedial-reading programs, continue to argue about the speed-reading method with each other and with speed-reading specialists. Those on each side of the controversy can muster eye specialists and psychologists to challenge the other, but there are big doses of self interest in all the arguments.

And after a person successfully takes a reading course and discovers he can't zip through the newspaper in 10 minutes, read historic-site markers from his moving car, or routinely best office mates in the race to digest the latest bulletin-board notice, he tends to avoid his friends' questions about speed reading. So do those who took courses and made little progress.

But—do the courses work?

Yes.

That is my conclusion. It rests on personal experience with speed reading and on talks with reading specialists at colleges, at the Department of Health, Education, and Welfare, and elsewhere. However, the "yes" needs qualification:

A speed-reading course taught by a competent instructor usually will help a co-operative student to double or triple his reading rate if the rate was fairly low at the start. It can help a student increase comprehension and help him learn to concentrate, for rapid-reading requires deep concentration.

A few students actually do appear able to read at 4,000 or 5,000 words a minute and to intelligently answer questions about the material later. But even these whizzes are unlikely to flash through the *Encyclopaedia Britannica* or Shakespeare's works in a day.

Despite advertisements to the contrary, the top speed readers cannot read everything at the same speed. They commonly adjust their pace to the toughness of the reading material and to their purpose. They may run through novels for pleasure, yet jog, or lumber, through material that other readers find relatively simple.

I began a speed-reading course offered by Bernard R. Hensley, a history teacher and art dealer in Alexandria, Va. Like most of the proliferating rapid-reading courses, his is an individually altered form of the innovative Evelyn Wood method.

I took Mr. Hensley's course because it is relatively inexpensive—$75 for eight, two-and-one-half hour sessions, contrasted with $225 for the equivalent Evelyn Wood offering. I was like most of the persons interested in such courses: They know they are slow readers; they have failed to make themselves faster on their own.

At the outset of the course, I read at the rate of 205 words per minute, a bit under the college graduate average of 250 to 300 w.p.m. Now I cannot comfortably drag along that slowly. Between 700 and 800 w.p.m. has become a comfortable rate using former techniques.

Using Mr. Hensley's method in the course's final exam, I read Sheila Burnford's *Incredible Journey* in a half hour to score 2,385 w.p.m. My comprehension, as based on results of a standard, high-school comprehension test for the novel: 92 per cent.

Reading that book wasn't satisfying. Hurtling through a novel allows no time for savoring clever phrases, or for doting on imagery. And the rapid reader often worries at the memory of passages he zoomed through without comprehending.

Mr. Hensley's stock answer to that worry: "That's a virtue. Read the book again, paying special attention to those passages. An hour is not too long to spend with a good book."

Rapid reading can be difficult and tiring. Much of the time spent in speed-reading classes and in the mandatory home practices is devoted to eye conditioning exercises or "eye calisthenics," which, Mr. Hensley explains, "expose the nervous system to high speeds, and thus build up the reader's tolerance for speed." The exercises train the reader to see the width of a page while steadily moving the eyes from top to bottom of page after page.

Top speed-reading instructors demand that students drill on techniques all specialists agree on. Students must "brief" or "survey" the book they are to read, examining it cover to cover, to see what it is about, what topics it covers. The reader notes names, places, dates, and phrases that seem to stand out. He formulates questions to ask himself while reading. Then he reads, pushing himself to hurry while looking at every word in every line though he might think he is going too fast for the words to register.

Afterwards the reader asks himself if he answered the questions raised before the reading. Often he must take a turn reporting to his speed-reading class the results of his briefing, questioning, reading, and reviewing.

It is this practice that eventually can double or triple reading speed. Yet if the doubling or tripling doesn't yield speeds of 1,000 or more w.p.m., the student isn't speed reading.

At 900 w.p.m. and lower the reader can "subvocalize," which means he can silently pronounce in his mind or even with his lips or in his throat the words he reads. Instructors say this sort of thing is the security blanket that trips students.

Teachers try to rid readers of subvocalization so the words will "flow directly into the mind." In an advertisement, one speed reader describes the process as akin to watching a film. He says there's no feeling of reading; involvement is so great the reader mentally sees the drama or string of ideas unfold.

On that point many who have successfully finished speed courses rebel. They fret about reading without "the feeling of reading," because they don't mentally experience the sense of having the drama unfold. They feel they have no evidence of having read intelligently except for a grade on a test, which, like all tests, is imperfect. Thus they tend to say speed reading, as defined by instructors, does not work, and they stop practicing it.

Never mind, say instructors; the method is always with you if you did, indeed, learn it. Whenever you decide to give the method a chance, you can start eye exercising, refer to class notes, and start speed reading again.

To test that assertion and to discover if I could mentally see the drama unfold this time, I returned to the instructor for another examination. I had used the speed-reading method just two or three times since the course ended a year and a half ago, and not at all recently.

Mr. Hensley ran me through seven or eight minutes of his eye calisthenics, allowed five minutes for briefing, then told me to read John Steinbeck's novel *The Pearl* in 15 minutes. I did, scoring 1,911 w.p.m. at 82 per cent comprehension. But I did not mentally see the drama unfold.

The Pearl strikes me as a splendid tale. I plan to read it again—slower.

—AUGUST GRIBBIN

HOME-MOVIE fans interested in tying together several generations of the family should explore old snapshots for links to the past. Assemble a selection of pictures of, say, great-great grandfather, great grandfather, and old homes figuring in the family history. Then photograph the pictures at close range with a movie camera, exploring interesting details in each. A chronological series of such shots can then be followed by shots of living members of the family and present homes. Sometimes it is possible to use this technique to tie together possibly six successive generations.

RECORDINGS ON TAPE are less susceptible to damage by scratching or wear than disc recordings. Care should be taken, however, in handling tapes, particularly those played with simple reels. Ampex Corp., a major manufacturer, suggests storage within the same ranges of temperature and humidity that people find comfortable and protection from dust and dirt. Reels should be allowed to come to a gentle stop, and they should be lifted by their hubs or lower flanges to avoid contacting the tape itself. Wrinkled and damage tape should be removed.

College –
The Road to Admission

CHOOSING a college used to be something a student started in his senior year at high school. Parents and students would do well to start the selection and preparation process as early as the ninth grade.

At the ninth-grade level it is important to make as firm a decision as possible on whether to seek college admission. If the decision is to try for college, careful tailoring of courses should begin.

Many colleges and universities are moving away from strict high-school course requirements. But many suggest this outline: four years of English; at least two years of a foreign language, with three years preferred; two or three years of social studies, with emphasis on American and European history; three years of mathematics, including two of algebra and one of plane geometry; and two years of science, preferably chemistry and physics.

In the 11th grade year, begin investigating some of the more than 2,480 degree-granting colleges and universities. Guidance counselors in high schools and private preparatory schools can help with information on tuition costs, acceptance requirements, enrolment size and character, library facilities, social regulations, and other important details. If adequate counseling is not available, one may have to rely on college admissions representatives who visit high schools periodically. Federally funded counseling centers are located in most large cities.

A service operated by the Association of College Admission Counselors (ACAC) can help a student find prospects among some 1,000 participating colleges. A student who has completed five semesters or more in high school should request an application from ACAC College Admissions Center, 801 Davis St., Evanston, Ill. 60201.

Their "Ask Us" service can save money. A $20 fee is required with application. But the process may cause many member colleges and universities to become aware of the applicant. Many will write him. The applicant then knows which colleges are interested in him. This can eliminate application payments, which average $15 for private institutions and $10 for public ones, to institutions that may have no interest in the applicant.

Library books also may guide you. *Comparative Guide to American Colleges,* by James Cass and Max Birnbaum (Harper and Row, Publisher, Inc., 49 E. 33rd St., New York City 10016; $8.95), will give you useful profiles and selectivity ratings. *Complete Planning for College,* by Sidney Sulkin (McGraw-Hill Book Co., Inc., 330 W. 42nd St., New York City 10036; $5.95), gives sound advice.

As choices are narrowed, weigh accreditation. It is easier to enter graduate school from an institution accredited by one of the six regional agencies: Western College Association, Northwest Association of Secondary and Higher Schools, North Central Association of Colleges and Secondary Schools, Southern Association of Colleges and Secondary Schools, or New England Association of Colleges and Secondary Schools.

Professional or technical institutions may be accredited by some 35 other agencies. Their names may be obtained from the Accreditation and Institution Eligibility Staff, U.S. Office of Education, Department of Health, Education, and Welfare, Washington, D.C. 20202.

Some nonaccredited institutions offer less-expensive programs. The Council for the Advancement of Small Colleges is made up of 105 colleges in 38 states. The colleges are working toward accreditation and some of their students have been admitted to graduate schools and the professions. For "A Directory of Member Colleges," send $1.50 to the council, Room 750, 1 Dupont Circle, N.W., Washington, D.C. 20036.

To learn more about any institution, arrange for an interview. This will allow one to question admissions personnel about their philosophies of education. Try to discover what they hope to make of their students. Avoid asking for answers already contained in brochures. Take the initiative; be the interviewer, not the interviewed.

Most colleges and universities require either the Scholastic Aptitude Test (SAT) or the American College Test (ACT) for admission. Information on the tests and registration materials is available at most high schools. Generally, it's best to take a Preliminary SAT in the junior year at a basic cost of $3; the SAT in the junior or senior year at a basic cost of $5.75, with as many as three achievement tests for an additional $8.75; and the ACT early in the senior year, at a basic cost of $6.

In the senior year, a student should apply to the desired colleges well before their deadlines. If financial aid is needed, pick up one of these forms at high school: a College Scholarship Service form for applicants to institutions that require the SAT, or a Family Financial Statement for institutions that require the ACT.

To seek aid from sources other than colleges or universities themselves, ask a counselor or teacher about funds provided by high-school organizations, church and civic groups, large corporations, and state and local governments.

Children of veterans of military service should read about possible educational assistance in a pamphlet entitled "Need a Lift?" Send 50 cents to the American Legion, P.O. Box 1055, Indianapolis, Ind. 64206.

WORK-AT-HOME schemes should be carefully scrutinized, warns the Council of Better Business Bureau, Inc. Advertisements, usually aimed at housewives, shut-ins, the elderly, and widows, typically suggest that the advertiser or some unspecified person will pay for work done in the home, such as sewing certain items. Often, says the CBBB, the advertiser's sole intent is to sell materials, kits, and instructions at high prices. Frequently there is little or no market for articles made with the kits. Legitimate concerns, says the CBBB, rarely require any payment or fees for materials utilized in work done for them in homes.

PAMPHLETS ON DRUGS and their dangers are available free from the National Institute of Mental Health as part of a public-information campaign. Written in question and answer form, the five pamphlets discuss marijuana, LSD, sedatives, stimulants, and narcotics, telling what they are, who uses them, and what the results might be. Another has answers to frequently asked questions about drugs. Single or multiple copies may be requested from NIMH, Box 1080, Washington, D.C. 20013.

Athletic Injuries

IF the family's young athlete is going out for football or any other contact sport this fall, he is subjecting himself to possible injury. But there are ways of minimizing injuries. They apply to players of almost any age in almost any sport.

Currently a major problem for football and soccer players is heat and humidity. High humidity on hot days does more than anything to bring about heat stroke and heat exhaustion.

According to Dr. Fred L. Allman, Jr., head of the Sports Medicine Clinic, Atlanta, past president of the American College of Sports Medicine, and consultant to the University of Georgia, six youths died of heat stroke in the first 10 days of the 1965 football season. Heat stroke has killed 39 players since 1931, and 24 of these deaths, mostly among young amateur players, have occurred since 1964.

To prevent heat casualties the doctor recommends "heat acclimatizing." It takes 10 to 14 days and involves:

Obtaining a careful medical history of players; limiting high-activity drills at first and increasing them gradually with, say, one 40-minute session the first day, one 50-minute session the next, and so on, providing 10 to 15 minutes of rest in each work hour, fitting players with loose, light clothes that readily absorb water; furnishing water and salt so heavily sweating players can replace fluids at each rest period; and being alert for such trouble signs as headache, nausea, unusually high fatigue, cramps, slowed mentality, and loss of co-ordination or awareness.

Emergency treatment for heat exhaustion or stroke requires immediately stripping the patient and cooling by fanning or by applying cool towels. The patient should have medical help as soon as possible.

The ankle sprain, bane of players in most sports, is the most common football injury, according to Marvin Roberson, athletic trainer at Brigham Young University, Provo, Utah, and editor of the National Athletic Trainers Association Journal. He explains that aside from exercising for prevention of sprains, trainers have begun using a method of ankle wrapping called "the Louisiana wrap." It can be applied by players themselves.

Even the standard "figure-eight" wrap explained in many first-aid manuals protects the ankle somewhat, but for details of the Louisiana wrap write: Cramer Products, Inc., Gardner, Kan. 66030. The company will send a free instruction sheet.

Cramer Products makes training supplies and accessories. It also publishes journals and brochures on treatment and prevention of sports mishaps. Recently it has collected many of these suggestions into a 72-page looseleaf book called *Athletic Training in Seventies*. It costs $4 and includes instructions for the Louisiana wrap.

According to Mr. Roberson, young athletes should know how to treat obvious sprains. He declares the first-aid treatment must start *"immediately* after the injury." He suggests the acronym "ICE" for remembering treatment, which, he says, often can bring a sprain under control within five days. "I" stands for immediate application of ice or some sort of cooling agent. "C" stands for "compression" or quick bandaging. And "E" stands for "elevation," of the injured area to reduce the flow of blood into the battered joint. If there is a suspicion of a bone injury the player should get prompt medical attention.

Some of the commonest injuries in contact sports and basketball also are among the most serious. They are shoulder separations and dislocations and knee injuries. Prevention requires special conditioning exercises that go beyond those normally demanded by coaches.

Dr. Allman explains that protecting bone joints requires muscle endurance, a product of running and swimming and to a lesser degree of cycling and hiking; muscle flexibility, the result of calisthenics; and muscle strength, a product of training with weights. Weight training means employing barbells and other paraphernalia while performing calisthenics-type exercises.

The athlete starts the training with as much weight as he can handle easily, then gradually adds more. The youngsters' common practice of piling on weight and hefting it to show their muscle prowess can be dangerous. It should be avoided. But every boy playing contact sports, even children 9 and 10 years old, should exercise with weights though the weights must be handled carefully.

Building shoulder muscle and seeing that shoulder pads fit properly are the best ways to guard against shoulder injuries. Complete weight-training programs, which include shoulder exercises, are common and can be obtained from books sold at athletic goods stores or borrowed from libraries.

In checking shoulder-pad fit, make sure the collar edge comes within one-half to three-quarters of an inch of the neck and that the hard, padded shell completely covers the collarbone and stretches to the shoulder.

Often the player himself must fit the pads before practice. He should take time to fit himself correctly.

Protecting the knee requires special tensing, flexing, and weight training, which utilizes weight boots that strap onto the foot and allow gradual addition of poundage. Dr. Allman and Dr. Karl K. Klein, another orthopedic specialist, have assembled the best, if not the only, exercising program designed for preventing knee injuries.

The various exercises, with photos and instructions for use of the weight boot, are contained in a scholarly work entitled *The Knee in Sports* (178 pages; $6.95). Copies may be obtained at some sporting goods stores and libraries or directly from the publisher, the Jenkins Publishing Co., 1 Pemberton Parkway, Austin, Texas 78703.

In the book, the doctors warn against three exercises commonly used for leg conditioning: deep knee bends, "duck waddles," and the full knee-bend squat jump. They all require lowering the body so the haunches drop below the knee joint. They can injure the knee joint. When performing bends or squats—with or without weights—the thighs should come parallel to the floor and no lower.

Dr. Allman believes youngsters should devote at least 15 to 30 minutes, three days a week to the special knee-protection drills. If all this seems a bit much to the kids, he says parents might tell them the leg conditioning can improve performance in games. It already has helped many college players and professionals.

DDT Substitutes

THE Government has moved to shut off DDT sales after reviewing studies indicating that the chemical can be harmful to man and game because of its persistence. However, other insecticides remain on the market that are effective and are deemed relatively safe. Any insecticide, of course, can prove dangerous, if used carelessly.

The safer insecticides will lose effectiveness after about 3 days; it may take DDT more than 20 years. The safer compounds break down before accumulating in plants or being assimilated into the body fat of animals. But their instability probably will make it necessary to apply them more often than DDT.

Here are some of the non-DDT insecticides:

✔ Carbaryl. Often sold as "Sevin," carbaryl will kill mosquitoes and many garden insects. But carbaryl can have the undesirable effect of killing honey bees.

✔ Diazinon. Kills hornets, cicadas, ants, cockroaches, silverfish, and other insects.

✔ Malathion. This is an especially popular substitute for DDT because it will kill an abundance of insects including mosquitoes, ants, fleas, silverfish, flies, and ticks. It also kills honey bees.

✔ Methoxychlor. This is closely related to DDT but is less toxic and decomposes more rapidly. It will kill mosquitoes, fleas, and other insects.

✔ Pyrethrins or natural insecticides derived from

daisylike plants found in Kenya. Natural and synthetic pyrethrins will kill mosquitoes, flies, and other insects.

These insecticides cannot be applied with labor-saving "fogging" devices. DDT could be placed in light oil that turned into a fog when dripped into a source of heat, such as the exhaust of a power mower. But the less-stable insecticides decompose too rapidly under heat to be spread in fog.

The non-DDT insecticides can be applied in several other ways. Insecticides in granules can be spread with small, hand-crank devices, which cost about $5. Dust insecticides come in squeeze dispensers. Liquid insecticides come in aerosol cans that cost about $1.50 to $2 for 10 or 12 ounces. And traditional, pump-action hand-sprayers that run about $1.50 to $5 will spread liquid insecticides over small areas.

More elaborate equipment is necessary for large areas. Granule insecticides can be spread in a device resembling a garden cart and costing from $9 to $97, depending on size and quality. Insecticides in the form of wettable powder or emulsifiable concentrate can be sprayed with attachments costing from $4 to $10 that fasten to the end of a garden hose.

Also available at from $10 to $45 are air-driven insecticide sprayers. Insecticide is dissolved in water in these tank sprayers and a built-in pump is used to increase air pressure in the tank. The pressure drives out an insecticide spray when a nozzle is triggered.

The key to shopping for insecticides is comparing the square area they will treat rather than the size of the packages that contain them. Concentrations of insecticides vary in wettable powders and emulsifiable concentrates. A product with a high concentration of insecticide and a low concentration of emulsifier can be mixed with water to cover a larger area than a product in the same-size container with a low concentration of insecticide.

Those who want to control insects without using any chemicals might consider the purple martin, a bird that regards mosquitoes as a delicacy and can be induced to homestead in a proper back-yard birdhouse. Or one may turn to the praying mantis, a comical insect that preys on plant-eating insects. Mantis eggs are available from the B & G Depot, Insect Control Center, 2 First St., East Norwalk, Conn. 06855. And even a praying mantis that won't eat his share of long-tailed mealy bugs is a fine conversation piece at a patio party.

THE BROWN RECLUSE SPIDER, whose bite is more dangerous than the black widow and whose venom, volume for volume, is more deadly than a rattlesnake's, is spreading throughout the United States. The National Safety Council says the shy, nocturnal insect has now migrated from the South into the Northern states and from the West into the Midwest. Though the brown recluse can be deadly, pain usually does not become severe for several hours after a bite. Extensive ulceration often results from nonfatal bites. The spider, about a half-inch long, is distinguished by a dark violin-shaped mark on its body. It frequents dark places, such as bedrolls, folded blankets, and packed clothing. Not aggressive, it usually does not bite unless pressed against the body. Prompt medical attention should be sought by anyone who suspects that a brown recluse has bitten him.

BOAT-TRAILER owners should have wheel bearings inspected frequently if they must back a trailer into water deep enough to reach the axle and hubs. Though the grease seals on most trailers are designed to be waterproof, the seal can be broken when a hub that is hot after high-speed highway travel is suddenly rolled into cold water. If water gets into the bearings, it can cause corrosion and break down protective grease. Where evidence of water is found, bearings and axle spindles should be wiped clean and repacked with fresh grease. When possible, try to avoid letting water reach trailer hubs.

Choosing a Nursing Home

F AMILIES of older persons often must weigh the alternative of using a nursing home against the feasibility of keeping an ailing or senile relative in their own homes. If they choose the nursing home, they are faced with the confusion of choosing among many institutions, which offer various combinations of services.

Facilities to care for the aged vary to accommodate differing needs. Some institutions accept persons who are in good health for their age; others will take those who require some supervision; and still others serve those who need constant attention.

About 50 institutions in the country combine all three functions. Bethany Home and Hospital of the Methodist Church in Chicago, for example, can accommodate some 600 people in apartments, an infirmary, or a general hospital.

Although some argue that entering a home catering to the sick could depress a healthy person, some geriatrics specialists feel that multi-purpose homes are the answer to the problems of the aging, whose health inevitably will decline. Most older persons feel a jolt no matter what type of institution they enter. Facilities with a variety of types of care may eliminate the shock of still another transfer.

Residents of nursing homes should, where possible, be near their families and friends. A state board of health can tell you if there is a consolidated nursing home like Bethany in your area. If none is nearby, you should consider the smaller, specialized institutions that are closer to home. Social-service agencies in large cities can help find them.

The ideal care in a nursing home should cost about $20 a day, according to Edna Nicholson, a medical-assistance consultant to the Department of Health, Education, and Welfare in Washington, D.C. But she says that most people pay from $10 to $15 a day, often receiving service below the ideal.

After locating several nearby nursing homes in your price range, you should visit each, keeping in mind the personal preferences and social needs of the prospective patient.

A quick look at an institution will give you a good idea of its level of comfort. But beware of making rapid judgments on social atmosphere: A home that is a model of tidiness may be that way because it severely restricts what residents may do in decorating their quarters.

Some physical characteristics are good indices of whether the home is livable. Residents should have space they can use outside their bedrooms such as a sun room or a recreation room. The area should be comfortable and not just a showcase.

The attitudes of the management staff and the residents are the best measure of the quality of the institution. A good test is to observe the expressions of the residents when staff members are present.

The conduct of the manager can indicate whether the residents are treated courteously: Do staff members knock before entering a room? Do they refer to residents as "Mr. Smith" or "Mrs. Smith"? Be wary if the method of address seems overly casual or informal.

The level of activity in a home is important. Some

nursing homes have occupational-therapy programs. Those that don't should at least have activity programs to entertain the residents and make them feel useful.

A person who likes a crowd should enter a home where group participation is encouraged. A more independent person should elect a home where, if he desires, he is free to keep to himself and pursue his own interests.

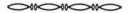

THE BLIND will be able to "read" talking books at twice the former possible speed with a new recording technique developed by the American Foundation for the Blind, 15 W. 16th St., New York City 10011, with co-operation by Bell Telephone Laboratories. The technique makes it possible to reproduce recorded speech at twice the speed at which it was spoken without producing the "Donald Duck" babble that results when a record or tape is simply speeded up. The technique, soon to be used in producing the free recordings of readings of books distributed to the blind by the Library of Congress, approximates the 300-to-400-words-per-minute rate at which many sighted persons speed read printed matter.

"TALKING BOOKS" are available to the blind in cassette-tape form from the Library of Congress, Washington, D.C. 20542. Both cassettes and portable playback devices may be borrowed at no charge from the library or 97 co-operating lending agencies throughout the country. The library has long made available readings of books on conventional phonograph records. Cassette players, however, are more readily used by the blind.

ARTHRITIS SUFFERERS, confused about the use of aspirin to ease pain and inflammation, may find some helpful information in a pamphlet, "The Truth About Aspirin for Arthritis," available free from the Arthritis Foundation, Box 2535, New York City 10001, and from local Foundation offices.

Sun Glasses – A Clearer View

AMERICANS apparently have a penchant for cheap, voguish sunglasses—exactly the kind that provide least comfort and most potential harm.

Estimates based on recent sales records indicate that vendors sell more than 150,000,000 pairs of sunglasses. About 57 per cent are bottom-of-the-line models, 99-cent to $3 items sold in supermarkets, drugstores, hardware shops, even at roadside stands.

Many of these cheaper brands fit poorly. Some are flimsy, unevenly colored, and so light they won't properly block unwanted sunlight. A few have highly flammable frames and are dangerous.

Still, some low-priced glasses are true bargains. And there are ways for the buyer with a bit of background about the product to spot a good buy, or at least to locate sunglasses that more nearly will do what's wanted.

The prime purpose of sunglasses is to make wearers comfortable in strong sunlight. Besides, they help motorists, boaters, and skiers to function more safely in glare. They also enhance night vision, which can be reduced 50 per cent by day-long exposure to bright sunlight. And, sunglasses with strong plastic or hardened "shatter-proof" lenses serve as shields for the eyes.

To do the job normally expected of them, sunglasses should be dark enough to block 80 per cent of the light. They should be two millimeters thick. They should have smooth, polished lenses that won't distort viewed objects. They should be of a "neutral" color, one that won't hamper recognition of other colors—for instance the red and green of traffic lights.

Generally, gray, the "smoked-glass color," is best. It's also the hardest to manufacture. So it costs more. Green is a good second choice.

Sunglasses using brilliant, primary colors can interfere with color identification. Despite common belief, there is no known color that will reduce the glare of oncoming automobile headlights in night driving without simultaneously distorting color perception and diminishing vision dangerously.

Mod "cosmetic glasses," as they're called, often don't qualify as sunglasses at all. Their tints are too pale. They screen out just about a quarter of the light true sunglasses should block. They generally are the wrong colors too. This is not to say they are harmful. They aren't. But they should not be expected to serve as sunglasses.

There are three principal kinds of sunglasses: absorptive, polarizing, and coated. The absorptive are the old, traditional kind. They function by soaking up ultraviolet and infrared rays.

Polarizing glasses admit to the eye light rays coming from one direction only. Thus they eliminate glare, the bouncing reflections from water, snow, and polished surfaces. They permit fishermen wearing them to peer down into a river that's glinting with reflected light.

Coated lenses have a metallic covering and themselves reflect light. Often they are absorptive lenses with what look like mirrors covering the outside of the lenses.

Most polarized lenses sold in the United States are plastic. Some of the strongest, toughest spectacles use plastic lenses. But plastic has a couple of drawbacks. It doesn't totally filter out the heat-producing infrared rays. So plastic glasses are hotter in summer, and sunbathers dozing face up to the sun could wake with irritated eyes and eyelids. Then too, plastic can be scratched more easily than glass. Plastic lenses must be cleaned with caution.

Glass isn't perfect either. It is indeed cooler in summer, but in winter it fogs readily.

The buyer who wants glasses for general wear isn't limited to one or the other though. Many manufacturers, including old-line companies like American Optical Co., Southbridge, Mass., and Bausch & Lomb, Inc., Rochester, N.Y., are now producing "sandwich glasses." These have a slice of polarizing plastic between two layers of regular absorptive glass. They function well overall, though they don't eliminate glare so well as pure polarizing lenses, nor do they soak up so much light as pure absorptive lenses.

Monaco Optical Corp., a division of Rayex Corp., New York City, markets photochromatic lenses, which are chemically treated so they change color according to the brightness of the light they are exposed to. Monaco calls its photochromatic glasses "Astro-matic glasses." They turn from light amber to smoky gray as the intensity of light striking them increases, and revert back to amber as the power of the light wanes. Theoretically they make it unnecessary to take glasses on and off when moving from bright to shady areas. They sell for from $3 to $10.

Sunglass frames are important too, if only because a few are potentially hazardous. Those made of cellulose nitrate will explode into flames if brought too close to a wavering match or cigaret lighter or if touched by a spark from an outdoor grill. Because they are so flammable, U.S. manufacturers stopped making them years ago. They are still around though, mainly on cheaper sunglasses imported from Germany and Italy.

It's hard to tell cellulose frames from others. One way is to sniff at the frames. If they have a camphor odor, they may be made of cellulose, for camphor is used in its manufacture.

There are other tests the buyer can make to ensure he's getting a quality product.

✔ Hold the glasses up to the light and see if they are perfectly clear, free of crisscross lines, scratches, streaks, and bubbles. Cheap lenses are made of blown glass, and often contain imperfections.

✔ Hold the glasses about a foot from the eyes. Looking through them, examine an object with strong vertical and horizontal lines—a window or door jamb. Move the glasses, up, down, and sideways. If the lines of the object appear to waver, reject the glasses. They are distorted. This doesn't apply to prescription lenses, which are intentionally distorted to improve vision.

✔ When possible, check the glasses outside the store in bright sunlight to see if they are sufficiently dark. Lenses that appear dark in artificial light may give little protection outside.

✔ Get glasses with big lenses. Prescription sunglasses should contain lenses a size larger than regular ones if they are to filter correctly light coming from the sides.

To see if a lens is large enough, cup your hands around it while standing in bright light. If this improves vision, the glasses should be rejected: They aren't providing adequate side shielding.

✔ Put on the glasses. Look in a mirror, checking to see if the pupil of the eye is close to the center of the lens. If it isn't, the glasses fit badly.

✔ Avoid glasses that easily slip down the nose. Properly fitting glasses bring the lenses close and hold them there. However, the lenses shouldn't be so close that the eyelashes brush them. Eyelashes can keep lenses constantly smeared.

✔ Don't use sunglasses with wide frames. They obscure peripheral vision. California law makes it illegal to sell in that state sunglasses with frames more than a half-inch wide. This is a good width to consider the maximum.

✔ Check the side pieces where they are hinged to the lens frame. Inferior glasses often are hinged with a simple pin instead of a screw or rivet.

✔ Look for an indication on the sunglass' label that indicates the lenses are "heat hardened" or "heat treated." Heat-hardened glass is "shatter-proof" glass. If the label doesn't say, ask the dealer if the lenses are shatter-proof. In an accident lenses that break and splinter can cost the wearer his eyesight.

Specialists agree that even the best sunglasses hinder rather than help persons who wear them habitually —in dark as well as in sunlight. The glasses can reduce the eye's tolerance to bright light, making it painful when he finally removes the glasses. Too, sunglasses reduce vision in twilight. That's an obvious handicap when driving.

LIGHTWEIGHT CLOTHING tends to catch fire more readily than most heavier winter garb, warns the National Fire Protection Association. The association reports that 6,500 persons die each year from clothing fires, and it cautions anew that it is best to stand clear of bonfires and barbecues—especially when wearing loosely fitting garments.

Getting Eyeglasses Fitted

ONE of every two Americans wear eyeglasses to correct his vision. By 1975, as people live longer and give greater value to good vision, two out of three are expected to be wearing glasses. A recent survey shows that there are about 15,000,000 persons who need glasses but don't have them. And another 21,000,000 should have new prescriptions for the glasses they are now wearing.

Despite the increasing prevalence of corrective lenses, few people fully understand what is meant by protective eyewear, or how ophthalmologists, optometrists, and opticians differ.

A child's first eye test may come during grade school when a nurse or volunteer asks him to indicate what he sees on a wall chart, a test primarily of distant vision. If he has difficulty, he may be referred to an eye specialist for further tests. Such a mass screening is limited, so parents and teachers should watch for other signs of poor vision: blinking more than normal, rubbing eyes frequently, squinting, trying to brush away a blur, excessive frowning, red or inflamed eyes. Children seldom complain of poor eyesight, because they don't realize how good it should be.

For the most thorough medical examination of a child or adult it is best to visit an ophthalmologist, a medical doctor with postgraduate training in eye diseases and surgery. He can detect not only structural eye problems that cause nearsightedness, farsightedness, or astigmatism, but also other medical disorders in the eye and elsewhere that affect vision. But ophthalmologists, sometimes called oculists, are in fairly short supply, so a family may want to seek alternatives.

Some family doctors have the training and equipment to examine eyes and give eyeglass prescriptions. There are also a few eye, ear, nose and throat specialists left who do this, although most of them have narrowed their work to just one or two fields.

Optometrists are not medical doctors. They do have five or six years of training after high school and hold doctor of optometry degrees. They are licensed by states to examine eyes and prescribe glasses. Most will refer patients to an ophthalmologist or other medical doctor if they suspect the presence of a disease.

About 40 per cent of the country's 8,500 ophthalmologists dispense as well as prescribe eyeglasses. The remainder refer patients to opticians, who usually buy standard lenses from a wholesale dealer, then perform a final grinding and polishing to make lenses conform to individual prescriptions and to frames selected by the customer. Most of the nation's 20,500 optometrists provide eyeglasses as part of their service, doing the work of the optician in their own offices or laboratories.

Unless the buyer specifies otherwise, the lenses of his new glasses probably will be unhardened crown glass, which can splinter into tiny, sharp fragments if hit with a hard object. Thousands of persons have lost their eyesight through injury from such glasses. Despite the danger, three-fourths of the corrective lenses sold today are unhardened glass.

Protective or safety lenses are either plastic or are hardened glass, which is heated to 1,330 degrees Fahrenheit and then cooled quickly in cold air or oil. Hardened glass, required in all new automobile windows, will withstand a greater impact before breaking and form small pieces with rounded edges when it does break.

Safety lenses may be slightly thicker than ordinary lenses. To reduce weight, a person can buy lighter frames or get plastic lenses instead of glass. Plastic weighs half as much and is at least twice as impact resistant as hardened glass. It scratches easily, however, and must be handled more carefully.

Protective lenses may cost from $2 to $4 more per pair than unhardened glass. They are well worth the cost, especially for active children.

Imported plastic frames or domestic frames manufactured more than 10 years ago may be made from cellulose nitrate, which can burn rapidly. There is no easy way to tell the difference between it and acetate, which has been used in this country for 10 years and now is common among imported frames. A specialist selling new frames should be able to tell you which ones are safe.

The costs of eye examinations and eyewear vary with the geographic location, type of lenses, frames, examiner, and seller. Single-focal lenses may cost from $12 to $15 a pair; frames another $12 to $16. An ophthalmologist's fee most frequently is between $15 and $20, making the total cost for glasses somewhere between $39 and $51. An optometrist's total fee for examination and glasses may be slightly lower, depending on the services he performs and his source for the glasses.

Contact lenses cost considerably more; they also require several trips to the seller's office for fitting and follow-up examinations. The cost usually ranges from $150 to $200 when all specialists' fees and insurance against loss are included. New "soft" contact lenses cost even more.

There are many optometrists and opticians who

advertise discount prices for eye examinations and glasses. This is an area with few government regulations and one should be wary of bargain-basement prices. To save costs, the eyeglass discounter may give an incomplete examination or be careless in grinding a prescription or adjusting lenses and frames to a patient. He may also sell poorly made and flammable frames. Discount-priced contact lenses are especially subject to variations that can be medically dangerous.

Yet savings are available from some reliable merchants who sell top quality lenses and frames. Opinions from family doctors and ophthalmologists can help locate good buys. Doctors learn about prices and reliability from their many patients' experiences and may offer recommendations. And a person should not hesitate to take his new glasses back to an ophthalmologist for examination; most will not charge another fee if they issued the prescription.

FORGERY INSURANCE is offered as part of some homeowner policies or as optional coverage. Insurance buyers should understand, before paying extra for such coverage, that they are almost never liable for forged personal checks, providing they notice the forgery on canceled checks and promptly notify the bank. Forgery insurance might cover legal fees, however, when there is some question of negligence on the part of the insured and a lawsuit is started to resolve it.

WATCH OUT for bills for merchandise or for publications renewals that are not really bills. An increasing number of solicitations, which are almost identical in appearance to bills, are turning up in the mails. A casual bill payer may get trapped into sending a check under the impression that he or his spouse ordered the item involved and then forgot about the order. Some states are considering legislation to outlaw mail solicitations that closely resemble bills.

Apartment Fire Hazards

 I F a fire occurs in a house it is usually caused directly or indirectly by some member of the resident family. But occupants of apartments and town houses or row houses sometimes are endangered by fire originating in another family's quarters. Both the National Fire Protection Association, headquartered in Boston, and the National Safety Council, headquartered in Chicago, recommend a number of fire-safety factors to watch for when shopping for housing in a multiple dwelling unit.

 ✔ There should be an enclosed stairway no farther than 50 feet from an apartment. Outdoor stairways are impractical; tenants using them to escape may be injured by fire flaring from windows or may fall during icy weather.

 ✔ A second enclosed stairway should be available that is far enough from the first so that if one is blocked, the other may be reached.

 ✔ Metal fire doors should insulate each floor from stairwells, which can act as fiery chimneys.

 ✔ Windows in rooms on the first three floors should be large enough to allow tenants to climb to safety.

 ✔ Balconies should be wider than the doors or glass panels opening onto them. The balcony area beyond doors and panels might afford safety for a person forced to flee from a burning room.

 ✔ Look for well-kept corridor and storage space.

Combustible trash should not be allowed to accumulate. Storage areas should be away from major stairways.

If fire breaks out in an apartment complex, here are recommended steps from the two safety organizations:

✓ Feel the apartment door. If it's cool, stand behind it and open it cautiously, bracing to slam it shut if there are flames or gases outside.

✓ If fire is blocking exits, or if it's hard to determine the location of the fire in a high-rise apartment, it may be safer to stay inside and call the fire department, the National Safety Council warns. Stuff damp blankets or towels in cracks around the door. Then get as far away from the door as possible, shutting other doors inside the apartment. Take refuge in a room with a window that may be opened slightly for ventilation. Hang a sheet outside to signal distress. If fire enters the apartment, seek shelter and fresh air on a balcony, or if worse comes to worst, huddle inside under the wet carpets or blankets.

SECOND-LOT OWNERS who are shopping around for an inexpensive shelter to put on it may be interested in the O'Dome, an ellipsoid-shaped shelter assembled from panels of laminated fiber board or glass-fiber foam. O'Domes, manufactured by Tension Structures, Inc., Box 217, Ann Arbor, Mich. 48107, come in 15-, 20-, and 25-foot diameters. Prices range from about $1,400 to about $3,500, freight included, and weight varies from 1,000 to 1,700 pounds. The panels lock together under tension and, says the manufacturer, can be assembled on a wooden deck in a day. The shelters may also be dismanteled for moving to another site.

Double-Drug Dangers

A PATIENT with heart disease is treated by a cardiologist who prescribes a drug to reduce blood coagulation. Later, in a period of nervous tension, the person seeks help from another physician who prescribes a barbiturate without being aware that the patient is taking the anticoagulant drug. The second drug may nullify the first, making the patient more prone to a fatal heart attack.

The problem of serious interaction between two drugs, each of them beneficial when taken alone, is a growing one. Public-health officials are beginning to issue warnings that all physicians treating a patient should be advised of all the drugs, prescription or otherwise, that the patient is taking.

Such a common household remedy as aspirin, for example, may cause severe hemorrhaging if taken by a patient also taking an anticoagulant. Dr. Arthur Ruskin, U.S. Food and Drug Administration (FDA) in Washington, D.C., says aspirin has also been known to increase the action of some drugs, other than insulin, used in treating diabetes, sometimes causing a patient to go into a coma.

Much about drug interaction is not understood. The complex interactions vary from person to person. Some drugs also impede the action of other drugs.

Scientists do have some ideas, though, about the way combinations of drugs are likely to act on users.

Antacids, taken to ease indigestion, sometimes

hamper the action of antibiotics used to check infectious diseases, according to Dr. Thomas H. Hayes, former head of the drug division of the American Medical Association in Chicago. The antacids believed primarily responsible for this type of interaction contain some form of aluminum hydroxide, he says.

Similarly, the effectiveness of anticoagulants may be blocked by some depressants, including barbiturates, Dr. Ruskin says. Taken to calm nerves or induce sleep, barbiturates speed the destruction in the liver of anticoagulants and may offset blood-clotting capabilities.

Dr. Ruskin believes it's wise for anyone taking barbiturates to refrain from using insecticides or pesticides, since there's evidence that some garden sprays, inhaled or absorbed through the skin, may interfere with the functioning of barbiturates.

Severe problems may also result when one drug enhances the effectiveness of another.

Physicians agree generally that stimulants, taken to keep a user awake or to combat depression, may have an exaggerated effect in conjunction with food or beverages containing a substance known as tyramine, commonly found in chicken livers, fava beans (served often in Italy), certain varieties of cheese, and alcohol. Thus a stimulant taken in the course of an evening in which cheese and wine are consumed could cause convulsions.

Alcohol intensifies the influence of depressants, including tranquilizers, sedatives, narcotic painkillers such as morphine and codeine (sometimes found in cough medicine), and antihistamines used to fight hay fever and other allergies. The combined effect of alcohol with a depressant may cause a coma.

So keep your physicians posted on all the drugs you are taking and solicit their advice.

Contact Lenses

REPLACING conventional eyeglasses with contact lenses is a gamble. There is no sure way to predict whether a person will be able to tolerate the lenses, which fit on the eyeballs. The wearer may achieve optimum vision without cumbersome spectacles or he may get constant irritation and more restricted vision.

New "soft" contact lenses, which are pliable, may be more comfortable than firm lenses. However, they are more expensive and mar more easily. Firm contact lenses likely will cost from $150 to $200. That is the common range for eye examinations, fittings, follow-up visits, and accessory items. The cost is higher for bifocal or other complex lenses.

Contact lenses are made of plastic, molded to fit the contour of each eye. Most persons, once they have adjusted to the lenses, wear them all day, removing them at night and for periodic cleaning.

The fitting of contact lenses is a precise procedure. Each lens is custom-made for a particular eye. Here is what is involved:

An examination is made to determine whether there are any medical or personal reasons why a particular patient should not try to wear contacts. If there are none, a prescription is issued for corrective contact lenses.

The external shape of each eye then is measured to determine the proper curvature for the contacts. They must cling to the eyes but still allow eye fluids to flow underneath. An instrument measures light reflected from the eye surface to gauge its radius of curvature.

The lenses are manufactured and given to the patient. He is shown how to put in and remove the lenses and told how to care for them. A specific wearing schedule is provided, beginning with just one or two hours the first day and gradually increasing.

Follow-up visits, perhaps twice a week at first and eventually every six months or so, are necessary to make sure the lenses are not causing eye damage or unnecessary discomfort. Often the lenses are adjusted slightly to improve their performance.

If you are considering contact lenses, it is important to decide how badly you want them. Strong determination is needed to get past the period of initial use, a most uncomfortable time. Tears flow freely. The first few days usually are the worst, but many persons have remained uncomfortable for weeks or months.

Women — who own about two-thirds of the estimated 7,000,000 sets of contact lenses that have been sold—and teen-agers have the best success records with contacts. The prime motivation among women is the wish to appear in public without glasses, and they tend to put up with the frequent inconveniences and discomfort to gain this benefit. Teenagers, whatever their motivations, find it easier than most to adjust to the lenses.

Men should look doubly hard at their motivations, for they usually have the hardest time adjusting to the lenses. A man may have the same desire as a woman to improve his appearance; if his desire is great enough it will be helpful. He may want very much to end the problems of eyeglasses slipping, steaming up, or getting wet from perspiration during strenuous activities. Contact lenses will rid him of these problems, but there also may be the new problem of losing lenses during such activities. And a contact lens, once it has popped out on a field or grassy area, probably is lost. The cost of replacement may be more than $50 without some form of insurance.

Contact lenses can improve vision greatly. They refract all light going into the eye, so there is no blurred peripheral vision as with regular lenses. But that advantage can be offset by a smoky room or polluted city air.

The eyes tire from contact lenses toward the end of the day, producing irritation similar to that from dust or smoke. The irritation becomes worse when the wearing time exceeds that of the previous day by even an hour or two. Thus a person must wear the lenses about the same length of time every day.

Wearing contacts would not be so troublesome if a person could switch easily to regular glasses and back. But the necessity of maintaining a constant wearing schedule precludes frequent switching and there is the additional problem that a person cannot see as well at first with regular glasses because the contacts tend to flatten the outer portion of the eye and alter the transmission of light.

Contact lenses are sold by opticians, ophthalmologists, and optometrists. Opticians are technologists who supply lenses to conform to a prescription. Opticians who sell contacts are able to measure the shape of an eye to fit a lens. But they ordinarily are not trained to determine the refraction needed in the lens. Opticians require a previous examination and prescription from someone, usually an ophthalmologist, who is trained to determine how lenses for particular eyes should be shaped.

Ophthalmologists are medical doctors with specialized training in diagnosing and treating eye diseases. They may work with opticians in fitting contact lenses or may fit the lenses themselves. In some areas, laws prohibit opticians from dispensing contacts or restrict them from doing so unless they are under the close supervision of an ophthalmologist.

Optometrists' training falls in between that of opticians and ophthalmologists, while their services generally encompass both areas. They are not medical doctors, but have training in recognizing eye diseases. Their ability both to measure refraction requirements and furnish the lenses to meet those requirements is a convenience for patients.

Experts familiar with all brands of lenses, say that one is about the same as another, so that the buyer need not be overly concerned about manufacturers' names.

In considering costs, determine the answers to these questions:

✔ Does the fee include an eye examination for a prescription? If not, what additional cost will there be for an examination by an optometrist or ophthalmologist?

✔ Is there an extra charge for a soaking kit and the solutions needed for sterilizing and cleaning the lenses?

✔ Will there be additional charges for follow-up visits? Many plans include visits for six months or more, others for just three months. If you buy from an optician, plan for a second trip to an ophthalmologist after about six months. Even if you deal with an optometrist, you might want to visit an ophthalmologist at some point for a close medical examination.

✔ Will you get one pair of lenses or two? It is always a good idea to have a spare pair after you have adjusted to full-time wearing. If a second pair is not included in the price, how much would spares cost?

🗸 What is the replacement price for lost lenses? Most practitioners offer a type of loss insurance. Find out what the replacement price is with and without the insurance.

🗸 Will there be any refund if you decide you cannot make the adjustment to contacts and stop wearing them? Is the refund conditioned on the practitioner's opinion of your ability to wear them as well as yours? Such refunds are rare, but are worth asking about.

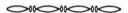

POWER WINDOWS on older cars have caused injury and death to small children playing unattended in vehicles, reports the National Safety Council. It is difficult for children playing in newer cars to harm themselves because the power-units are wired through the ignition switch and windows cannot be operated when the key is removed. The council suggests that parents of small children have the wiring on older cars similarly routed. The cost is estimated at around $15.

BARBECUE GRILLS should always be placed in a well-ventilated area if they are hurried into a home or tent ahead of a summer rainstorm. Burning charcoal gives off deadly carbon monoxide gas.

SHOE BUYERS should wait until they are tired and foot-sore from a day of shopping. Tired feet are relaxed, sensitive, and slightly broader than usual. A shoe that fits comfortably under those circumstances is most likely to remain comfortable under all other conditions.

A DIVORCED HUSBAND who makes payments to his former wife in return for her relinquishing any rights later to his retirement income cannot deduct such payments as alimony from Federal income-tax returns. The Internal Revenue Service, in ruling on the arrangement, also held that a former wife must treat such payments as income.

Shockproofing Rugs

HEAVY carpeting may make a room appear more luxurious. But it can also give an electrical shock to a person who touches a doorknob or light switch after walking across the carpet in cold weather. Some liquid products, however, make it possible to eliminate this sometimes unpleasant nuisance.

Rug shockproofing was first developed for institutional users, such as hotels, motels, and business offices. Because they have more carpeting than most individual homes, they have more of a problem with static electricity.

The carpeting at the Jacksonville (Fla.) International Airport, "was really shocking the fire out of us," says an airport official. A spray-on substance, he says, eliminated the problem with no harm to the rugs.

Static electricity can be a nuisance to machines as well as to individuals. One data-processing firm found that its computers were giving incorrect readings because of static-electricity build-ups induced by office carpeting.

The build-ups become a problem in cold weather, when the air in buildings often becomes dry and thus a poor conductor of electricity. Static electricity, which normally would flow from individuals or machinery before becoming noticeable, builds up. It flows suddenly and unpleasantly when a conductor, such as a doorknob, is touched. The problem is negligible in warm weather because the air is more moist and is constantly helping discharge electricity.

Household humidifiers will ease the static electricity problem in winter. So will spraying a carpet lightly with water. But water can make a rug soggy and attract dirt. To get around this problem, the spray-on products are composed of volatile liquids and a substance that conducts electricity. The liquid evaporates after being sprayed on a rug, leaving behind the conducting substance in the form of a dry residue.

Most of the shockproofing materials will last for a winter unless traffic is unusually heavy. Dirt and grease from shoes and feet will reduce the efficiency of the residue in carrying off electricity. But dirt and grease themselves also carry off electricity, though less efficiently than the residue, so it is possible that a heavily used carpet will not need shockproofing treatment.

Determining the amount of shockproofing to be sprayed on a rug often is a matter of trial and error. One manufacturer suggests a light spraying to begin. Then test the degree of effectiveness by walking across the rug and touching a doorknob. If there is a shock, repeat light sprayings until it is eliminated. Be careful not to apply too much spray at a time or the carpet may become messy.

Manufacturers of rug shockproofing sprays include Bryn Mawr Products, Box 212, Bryn Mawr, Pa. 19010, whose product is called Anti-Static, and Lab Automated Chemicals, Howard and West Streets, Baltimore 21230, which produces No-Shock. A 20-ounce can of either product costs about $2.

Choosing a Homebuilder

IT pays these days to check extra carefully on the financial reserves of the builder if you are thinking of buying a new house. Otherwise you may not get the house and lot you sign up for—or even recover your down payment if something goes sour.

Such disappointments and financial losses can occur when a builder goes broke before completing your house. When this happens, you may well stand near the end of the line as far as getting your down payment back. Laborers, suppliers, and banks usually get first crack at whatever assets the builder may have left.

It's important to find out as much as you can about the builder. You should shy away from any who cannot satisfy you that he has adequate financing lined up to ensure completion of the project.

Builders who have their financing firmly lined up before starting construction rarely get into trouble. The problems usually come with builders who have enough resources to get a project started but not enough to complete it without depending on down payments from individual buyers as the work progresses.

If you have any doubt about a builder's financial situation, ask him how he is financing the house or development. See if your bank can help you get a line on the soundness of his financing. Check with the local Better Business Bureau to see if it has any reports of problems involving the builder.

If you have any reservations about the ability of

the builder to complete the home in a satisfactory manner, insist that your deposit be placed in escrow. In such an arrangement the money is held by a third party until the terms of the building contract are fulfilled.

You also can insist on a contract provision obligating the builder to return the deposit if he fails to deliver a marketable title to the house. This helps protect against unforeseen rights others might have in the real estate involved.

A lawyer, if one is hired, should be retained in time to check and advise on provisions in the sales contract. At the closing, when final payment is made and the deed is delivered, the lawyer should be on hand to check all documents.

There are many books available for potential home buyers. Jerome G. Rose, an attorney now teaching at Rutgers University, has written *The Legal Adviser on Home Ownership* (Little, Brown and Company, 34 Beacon St., Boston, Mass. 02106; $10; and Bantam Books, Inc., 271 Madison Ave., New York City 10016; $1). It is concerned mostly with buying and maintaining used houses, but also includes much useful data on buying new homes.

The Small Homes Council—Building Research Council, University of Illinois, 1 E. St. Mary's Rd., Champaign, Ill. 61820, will mail an 8-page circular "Business Dealings with Architect and Contractor" for 15 cents. A list of other publications for the home buyer and owner may also be requested.

Lawn Maintenance Companies

A GROWING number of companies is specializing in taking over the hardest parts of lawn care for those who would prefer to spend their spare time at more leisurely pursuits.

Though the range of services offered by these companies varies, most will rake and clean a lawn, reseed it, and provide periodic weed and insect control. A few even provide regular mowing service.

Some companies base price quotations on the number of square feet in a lawn; others contract on an hourly basis. Auto-Lawn of America, a franchise operation with headquarters in Wickatunk, N.J., charges about 3½ cents a square foot for four lawn treatments a year, including seeding, fertilizing, and insect and weed control. The minimum charge is $140, or the cost of a 4,000-square-foot lawn. Hourly rates vary widely from area to area. A company working on an hourly basis would have to provide a rather precise estimate of the time required to care for a lawn in order for a shopper to have an effective cost comparison with a company operating on a square-foot basis.

Anyone contemplating turning lawn maintenance over to a company should plan to come to a decision in time to reach an agreement two weeks to a month before the first work is done. This is to give the selected company time to work the lawn into its schedule.

Coffee–A Matter of Taste

THE coffee drinker could put away several cups in the time it takes to decide which coffee gives the best taste at the lowest cost. Complicating his problem is the establishment of freeze-dried coffee as a regular item on grocery shelves. There are now three basic types of coffee to choose from: nonsoluble, soluble or instant, and freeze-dried soluble.

While picking the most flavorful coffee is a matter of taste, choosing the most economical buy is simpler even though prices vary according to brands, geography, and local customs. In the Western states, for example, coffee usually is served weaker than in the East. Generally, though, a typical cup of freeze-dried coffee will cost about 2 cents; nonsoluble coffee about 1.6 cents; and instant coffee about 1.3 cents. Nonsoluble coffee packaged in paper bags usually is a little cheaper than that packed in cans.

Exotic coffee varieties are expensive, even in sacks. The quality of coffee is related to the altitude at which coffee trees grow—the higher the altitude, the more aromatic the coffee. Rain, produced as air currents rise along a mountain slope, influences the aroma. The best beans come from heights about 3,000 feet. Celebes-Kalossie from Indonesia is a favorite of connoisseurs. It is available at $2.65 a pound from Peet's Coffee, Tea & Spices, 2124 Vine St., Berkeley, Calif. 94709.

The United States imports more green or partially processed coffee than any other country. Green coffee is made from raw coffee by one of two methods. In the "dry" method, coffee cheeries or red berries, each containing two beans, are rinsed and dried. Later they are skinned. In the "wash" method, the cheeries are broken open first, then washed, dried, and polished.

Companies in this country roast the green coffee. If the more expensive wash method has been used, all chaff is gone. If not, it must be removed during roasting. Roasters will buy unwashed coffee if the types are good. Brazil coffee, for example, is a sweet unwashed type often mixed with bitter types in blends. Of the washed types, Colombian and Guatemalan are heavy coffees; Kona from Hawaii is light.

The flavor of any type of coffee is altered by roasting. Lengthy roasting makes stronger coffee. Many Latin Americans prefer coffee with bite; at the Brazilian Embassy in Washington, D.C., staff members drink straight Brazil coffee roasted dark. The strongest coffee of all is Espresso, made by roasting any type of coffee until the beans are almost black.

It is possible to roast your own coffee. Beans may be roasted in a pan, a non-electric roasting pot that sells for $8 to $10, or an electric pot that sells for about $45. It takes about 1½ hours to bring a pound of beans to medium darkness with home roasting equipment. Commercial equipment roasts beans in a flame and is much faster. But commercial roasters willing to handle small quantities are usually found only in larger cities.

Serious coffee fanciers advise buying coffee in bean form and grinding it yourself. Beans may be of one kind or packaged as blends. Grinding at home helps preserve the flavor contained in the volatile oil in the beans. Manual and electric home grinders are available for $6.50 to $30.

Instant coffee results when ground coffee is percolated and then dehydrated. It is percolated and then frozen to make freeze-dried coffee. The frozen coffee is put in a vacuum where the ice crystals sublimate or change from a solid to a vapor, which is removed, leaving dry coffee concentrate. Freeze-dried coffee was put on the market in 1968, some 22 years after instant coffee.

Caffein can be removed from any type of coffee. Extracted caffein is sold to pharmaceutical and other companies and often is used in headache compounds and pills that combat nervous system, respiratory, and cardiac disorders.

Three methods are usually used to brew coffee from nonsoluble ground beans. Most familiar is percolation. Another is steeping the coffee in hot water in a pot or covered saucepan. The third is allowing hot water to filter through finely ground coffee.

Many persons who take their coffee preparation seriously say coffee making should never involve boiling and for that reason discourage the use of a percolator. Boiling is said to drive off many desirable elements of coffee as gases and to retain some undesirable ones as liquids.

The best coffee containers are made of glass, porcelain, or stainless steel. Aluminum reacts chemically with coffee to produce a bad taste. All containers should be kept clean; if coffee oils are allowed to stay, they will sour. Baking soda is a good cleanser.

TIRE SHOPPERS should shy away from tires marked "Farm Use Only" for anything other than the indicated use. Tires so marked do not necessarily meet Federal minimum standards for tires intended for highway use. The National Highway Safety Bureau says it has indications that the special tires are being sold for passenger-car use and that some dealers and distributors are buffing off the restricted-use label.

What's Cooking in
Pots and Pans

WHEN you fry eggs, do you use a skillet made of steel, aluminum, glass ceramic, or iron? Do you know what differences the various substances make in cooking? Or why a set of shining aluminum pans with decorative copper handles offers a maximum of functional disadvantages?

If not, you're in good company. A housewares trade journal recently reported that even salespersons often don't know. So it isn't always easy to find out by asking questions when you buy.

Price isn't usually a major factor in deciding whether to buy similar aluminum, stainless steel, or another type of utensil; quality products in any of the materials will cost about the same. For example, about $14 to $18 for a 10-inch, covered skillet is the price range in best-quality utensils; about $3 to $9 for such a skillet is the range for lower quality in most metals.

In general, the heavier the metal, the better it will perform and the more durable—and expensive—it will be. It is especially true in cookware that spending a few dollars more for the best quality will be worth it; since the utensils are likely to last a long time, the extra cost will be spread over several years.

With few exceptions, good design and sturdy, heat-resistant (usually plastic) handles are standard.

It is true that each type of metal or glass ceramic can be used for most types of cooking, but each has specific strong points.

Aluminum ranks just below copper as an excellent conductor of heat. This means the bottom and sides of an aluminum utensil rapidly and evenly reach a uniform temperature, a special advantage in frying, browning, or boiling scorchable foods, such as puddings.

However, aluminum surfaces easily stain and discolor, and are porous, which means food will cling. So cleaning can be a problem. However, most manufacturers now offer even low-priced, thin-gauge utensils with some form of enamel, porcelain (fired-on glass), or polyimide (fired-on plastic) coatings in attractive colors; these surfaces are easy to clean.

Aluminum utensils also usually have some form of nonstick lining, most often Teflon or Teflon II, which facilitates cleaning and preserves appearances. Both the linings and coated exteriors can be soaked free of clinging foods, washed in a dishwasher, or cleaned in hot soapy water. But some care is required; neither should be cleaned with metal or highly abrasive cleansers.

In lighter weights, aluminum dents easily. Its thickness is measured in gauges: 8-gauge is about the thickest, 18-gauge is quite thin. The heaviest weight in aluminum cooking sets offers 8-gauge skillets, 10-gauge saucepans. The very inexpensive saucepans ($1 to $3) are sometimes as thin as 25-gauge.

In buying aluminum utensils, the best bet is a heavy gauge with nonstick linings and easy-to-clean outer coatings.

Stainless steel more or less reverses the qualities of aluminum: It has a hard, durable, easy-to-clean surface, but is a poor conductor of heat.

To overcome this disadvantage, these utensils are frequently manufactured with a "heat core," such as carbon steel, with stainless steel layers on both sides (called tri-ply) or with a layer of aluminum or copper added on the bottom of the pans. Although copper is slightly ahead of aluminum in heat conduction, it is a bit more difficult to keep clean. The clad bottoms seem somewhat more effective in spreading heat than the heat core alone.

Stainless-steel utensils are available with both porcelain exteriors and with nonstick linings. Except for the attractive appearance of the colored outer coating, both are really unnecessary, since stainless steel itself is a relatively nonstick surface and retains a good appearance when cleaned by any method. The inner or outer linings actually make more care necessary.

The best buy in stainless-steel utensils are heavy weight tri-ply pans with copper or aluminum bottoms and without the inner lining or outer coating.

Copper utensils are also available—usually a copper outside bonded to stainless steel interiors. They put the quick heat conduction of copper to work up the sides as well as across the bottom of the utensils, but are very expensive (10-inch skillet, about $23) and require considerable care to keep their shiny appearance.

Glass-ceramic utensils such as those made by Corning Ware, are available in utensils for every type of stove-top and oven cooking.

Glass-ceramic utensils are poor conductors but good retainers of heat. This makes them very good for oven use, but care is required to avoid spot-heating and scorching when they are used on a stove top. After the heat is turned off, the glass remains hot and continues to cook the food for several minutes.

Glass-ceramic surfaces are nonstick, and they do not absorb flavors and odors as other materials may do. Their detachable handles and resistance to temperature change make them favorable for cooking and then storing or serving foods.

Cast-iron utensils are historic favorites of chefs and cooks because of their slow, even heating. Cast iron has particular advantages in frying and broiling, since it holds heat well and is slow to scorch or burn foods. However, it is very heavy, and rusts easily when exposed to moisture. In its plain, uncoated form it should be seasoned occasionally (coated with fat, baked in the oven for about an hour at 280 degrees).

However, cast iron is also available with a porcelain coating inside and out, which eliminates rusting and the necessity for seasoning. Plain cast-iron utensils are among the cheapest on the market—$3 for a 10½-inch skillet; the coated cast iron is priced at the level of the other types of good-quality utensils.

In general, each kind of utensil comes with special instructions from the manufacturer for both cooking and cleaning. It is important to follow them, particularly with regard to the amount of heat to be used.

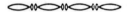

A COOLING AGENT that can be stored indefinitely in dry form, has been developed by the Chase Chemical Corp., 2646 Gulf Life Tower, Jacksonville, Fla. 32207. The chemical, packaged in a plastic container, drops to 12 to 14 degrees when fresh or salt water is added. Chase says a container of the product, called Ice-O-Magic, will keep the contents of an insulated picnic cooler chilled for about 24 hours if the contents were cool to begin with. The chemical, with a suggested retail price of about $1, is much more expensive than ice but can be used when and as needed.

FONDUE FANCIERS should be careful not to create a dangerous fire hazard, warns the National Safety Council. Some manufacturers sell fondue cooking oil with instructions saying that it is ready for use when it is hot enough to bubble. But, says the council, oil may become hot enough to flash into flame before it begins to bubble.

Tea Choosing

AMERICANS are second only to the British in the total amount of tea they drink. They pour down some 35 billion cups or glasses a year. Few, however, have sampled more than one of the three basic types of tea or as many as a half a dozen of the 3,000 varieties on the market.

The usual tea drinker makes his brew with a tea bag containing a mixture of "black" teas selected and packaged by one of the big five marketers: Lipton, Salada, Brooke Bond Foods, Inc. (Red Rose), Standard Brands, Inc. (Tender Leaf), and McCormick. These major brands and others found in most supermarkets tend to be similar in price and taste.

A far wider variety may be found in smaller specialty stores. With some basic information on what to look for and willingness to spend a little more money, venturesome tea drinkers can experiment with new tastes and perhaps discover a tea flavor that suits better than any they have sampled yet.

Teas fit into one of three general classes: black, green, and oolong, a Chinese term. The names have less to do with the appearance of the leaves or the brew they make than with the techniques used in processing them.

Black tea results when fresh leaves are dried, rolled, sifted, spread out in a cool, damp atmosphere to ferment, then redried, or "fired," to end fermentation. The process yields a leaf with a hearty flavor.

Green tea is prepared in somewhat the same way, but is not fermented. Oolong, which comes almost exclusively from Formosa, is fermented for a shorter period than black tea. It actually is semifermented and has a flavor that is weaker than black tea, stronger than green.

Like wines, teas are rated according to the country from which they come, often down to the region and tea garden from which they come. The product engenders the same sort of epicurean study and liturgy that wine does. The black teas generally rated best by the tea industry come from northern and southern areas of India and from Ceylon. Good blacks come from Indonesia, Africa, and Formosa. Japan provides highly regarded green teas; Formosa yields favored greens and the medium-strength oolong.

Various special names have become famous in the tea trade. They are normally reliable guides to quality. Each refers to a distinctive tea or tea blend.

Among the well-known names of stronger teas:

English Breakfast, a mixture of black teas grown in India and Ceylon; Darjeeling, a black, Indian tea raised near the city of Darjeeling, noted for its fullness, richness, and aroma, and recommended for use in iced tea because it retains its flavor despite dilution by ice; Lapsang souchong, a black Formosan with a deep, unusually smoky odor and flavor; and Earl Gray, a scented mixture of black teas from India and Ceylon blended in England.

Oolong, the Formosan tea, is among the lighter teas. Others:

Imperial Gunpowder, a green Formosan, with a delicate flavor, though it is among the stronger of the lighter teas; Young Hyson, another green Formosan, which is distinguished by its large leaf and dainty flavor; Jasmine, a black Formosan containing blossoms of the jasmine flower, and Basket Fired, green Japanese tea, which is light and gentle. Oolong and Jasmine are commonly served in U.S. Chinese restaurants.

Many unblended teas and English mixes can be bought at specialty-food stores or fancy-food sections of department stores and some supermarkets. While some of the imported teas sell for just a few cents more than U.S. brands, many are relatively expensive. For instance, a half pound of loose Darjeeling, one of the most costly teas, retails for about $1.70. A box of 48 Darjeeling tea bags goes for roughly 85 cents. A half pound of Lipton's tea sells for approximately 85 cents and 48 Lipton tea bags for about 65 cents. Prices vary somewhat from region to region and from store to store.

Though even the most revered imported teas come in bags now, specialists think that the bags make a less tasty brew than loose tea. They say that boiling water poured over loose tea causes the leaves to swirl about and give off more essence than leaf particles in a nearly motionless tea bag.

They also say Americans fail to get the most from tea for other reasons, declaring that Americans commonly let the tea steep too little or too much, that they fail to heat the teapot before brewing, and that they don't let the water come to a rolling boil before brewing.

Here are some tea-making tips gathered from the specialists and published by the Tea Council of the U.S.A., Inc., a New York City industry association.

For hot tea made in a teapot:

Wash out the teapot with hot water to warm it. This helps to prevent the pot from absorbing the heat from the water during brewing. Heat fresh, cold, faucet water until it reaches a bubbling boil—the "rolling boil." Use a single teaspoon of loose tea or one tea bag for each cup of tea to be made. Let the tea-water mixture steep for from three to five minutes. Don't just guess at the time. Use a clock. Brewing time is important. Of course, the longer the mixture brews the stronger it becomes.

For iced tea, use half again as much tea per cup as is required for hot tea—six teaspoons of loose tea or six tea bags for four glasses of iced tea, etc. Let the tea brew for the full five minutes. And don't fret about deterioration of taste if the concoction turns cloudy during refrigeration. Cloudiness doesn't affect taste. Restore the clearness by adding a small amount of boiling water. Better still, keep the mixture from clouding by letting the brew sit at room temperature before serving.

For a big batch of tea, make a concentrate that will yield 25 cups. Here's how:

Boil a quart of fresh, cold water. Add two-thirds of a cup of loose tea. Steep for the full five minutes. Stir, strain into a pitcher or teapot. Let the tea sit at room temperature until used, but no longer than four hours. Ladle out two tablespoons of concentrate into each cup of tea desired and fill the rest of the cup with hot water.

COMING ATTRACTION: Users of surgically implanted pacemakers, used to stimulate regular "beats" by some types of defective hearts, soon may be able to avoid periodical minor surgery to replace pacemaker batteries. Physicians working with Bell Telephone Laboratories, Murray Hill, N.J. 07974, have developed an experimental pacemaker that runs on electrical energy produced by blood pressure. It utilizes devices called piezoelectric discs, which convert pressure to electricity. The experimental pacemaker stores enough pressure-generated electricity to provide stimulation to the heart should it stop beating, thus causing a drop in blood pressure.

Oriental Rugs Need
Careful Selection

AMERICANS spend nearly $50,000,000 a year on the colorful floral- and geometric-patterned Oriental floor coverings that once were found primarily in the homes of the wealthy. Today they come in prices to fit all pocketbooks. But picking an Oriental is not like choosing a broadloom, so how is the average housewife to proceed?

First pick a reliable dealer, advises an officer of the Oriental Rug Importers Association of America. There are more than 150 kinds of Persian rugs alone, not to mention new rugs from India and Pakistan and historic old ones from Turkey, the Caucasus, and China and other Eastern areas. To learn the relative merits of all these rugs can take a lifetime. And most of the qualities that determine the value of an Oriental—fineness of weave, quality of wool, clarity of color—are invisible to the inexpert eye.

A novice buyer's best bet is to rely on someone she trusts. This may be someone she knows personally or a department-store dealer or Oriental-rug specialist who has been doing business in her community for a respectable number of years. It may even be an auctioneer of good reputation. But stay away from fly-by-night dealers: A poor quality Oriental at bargain prices is no bargain.

Oriental rugs have been coming to the United States since the Eighteenth Century, but most Americans still know little if anything about them. An Oriental, though there is no legal definition, is generally considered to be any hand-woven rug made east of the Suez Canal. American-made rugs of Oriental design, their exotic-sounding names always ending in "stan," do not qualify, nor do machine-woven rugs from industrialized Eastern areas. A buyer can usually tell a machine-made rug by checking the weave on the back: Machine-made weaves always are ruler straight; the rows of knots in a hand-woven rug never are.

Traditional Oriental rugs fall into six-well-defined categories named for the areas where the rugs were made: Turkish, Persian, Caucasian, Turkoman (often also called Bokhara rugs, and made in an area of central Asia populated mostly by nomads), Indian, and Chinese.

The vagaries of international politics and economics have eliminated the products of certain important rug-weaving areas from today's Western markets, while new areas have grown in importance since World War II. Rugs from the Caucasus now all go behind the Iron Curtain, for example, and the Bamboo Curtain successfully contains rugs from China.

Persia, which has reclaimed its ancient name of Iran, contributes more than 50 per cent of the rugs now being imported to the United States. Next are Indian rugs, which have leaped in popularity in the past five years, followed by rugs from Pakistan, a country that did not exist in the Golden Age of rug weaving in the Seventeenth and Eighteenth centuries.

Oriental rugs come in hundreds of sizes, designs, and colors, and practically all of them mean something. The sizes, for example, are determined by the size of the weaver's loom. Nomadic peoples always weave smaller rugs because their looms must be portable.

Certain designs and colors prevail in certain weaving areas. Many designs are historically or religiously important. Rugs woven in Moslem areas almost always are made up of arabesques because the Koran forbids the representation of living forms. Prayer rugs can be recognized by the geometric *mihrabs* woven into them, pointing the way to Mecca. Persians historically have meant their rugs to be indoor gardens, so that almost any Persian rug you see will be a mosaic of floral patterns. This is true even of the new Persians, which, in deference to Western tastes, often include a central medallion and a clear field of solid color around which the traditional Persian flowers are grouped in borders.

It is a common misconception that the plusher a rug, the better it is. This is not necessarily true of hand-woven Orientals. The more hand-tied knots that can be packed into a given space, the stronger the rug will be and the more intricate can be its design. Thus the finer the weave the higher the rug is valued in Oriental circles. This does not mean that coarse-woven rugs are not good, on the other hand. But new buyers would be wise to keep in mind this rule of thumb: "For equal durability, a fine woven rug may be thin, but a coarsely woven one must always be thick."

Whether it is better to buy an antique Oriental or a new one is a matter of taste. The rugs are basically made the same today as they were centuries ago. And it is not true that Orientals last forever, except perhaps in museum cases. An ancient unraveling Oriental—unless it is an example of a historically important rug that is no longer made—could be worth little, while a new Nain, a post-World War II Persian rug that many experts consider one of the most finely woven rugs ever to come out of Persia, probably will grow into a valuable antique.

Oriental rugs do last longer—if well made and properly cared for—than do most machine-made rugs.

So there are lots of old Orientals around. Though there is no legal definition, the Oriental Rug Importers Association has been trying to establish in general that an antique Oriental is a rug 100 years old or more; a semi-antique is one used in the Orient from 20 to 100 years; and a used Oriental is a rug used up to 100 years in the United States. Any rug with less than 20 years of wear in the Orient is still considered a new rug when it reaches these shores.

There are reasons for these divisions. In the Orient, rugs are trod on with bare feet so a particular kind of Oriental will wear out faster in the United States than will a comparable rug in the Orient. Also, an unused new rug likely will have harsher colors than an antique, since it is the years of constant shoeless wear that gives antique Orientals their rich, yellow colors and distinctive sheen.

Any number of books have been written about antique Orientals, but few of them also deal with the new types of rugs that have come on the market since World War II. One that does is Charles W. Jacobsen's *Oriental Rugs: A Complete Guide* (Charles E. Tuttle Co., Inc., Rutland, Vt.; $12.50) which is available in many public libraries.

RABIES is now reported about twice as often in wild animals as in domestic animals. Outdoor vacationers should be particularly wary of rabid skunks, which may make unprovoked attacks. The U.S. Center for Disease Control reports that skunks in one recent year accounted for 43 per cent of the 2,672 reported cases of rabies in wildlife; foxes and bats ranked second and third. Though only 11 cases of rabies are known to have developed in humans over the past seven years, some 30,000 persons each year take painful antirabies treatment following bites or scratches by known or suspected rabid animals.

A Basic Tool Set

A BASIC set of hand tools is becoming ever more essential for the homeowner as the ranks of handymen-for-hire continue to decline and the fees of those who remain continue to go up.

There isn't much agreement on what constitutes a basic tool set. But the following list represents something of a consensus by a few hardware dealers and veteran homeowners:

✔ Claw Hammer. It should have a forged-steel head and weigh 14 ounces. The lady who thinks that might be too heavy to heft can grip the hammer higher up on the handle. Acceptable models cost from about $2.75 up.

✔ Screwdriver. The most common model has a four-inch-long shaft and a one-quarter-inch tip. But a single screwdriver usually is inadequate for the variety of screws found in a home. Consider, then, a six- or seven-piece set. Besides a selection of conventional screwdrivers, it should have one with a very short handle for work in confined space and one or more with a Phillips or cross-shaped tip. Such sets cost about $3.00.

✔ Pliers. The most familiar ones are called "slip-joint" pliers. Forged-alloy or carbon-steel models are good. They cost about $1. But one pair of pliers won't do for long either. "Long-nose" pliers with a side cutter for snipping wire may be necessary. Cost: About $2. The "locking plier-wrench" that grips, clamps, and generally works like a vise costs about $2.25. "Water-pump" or "arc-joint" pliers, which have grooves to hold the adjustable jaws various distances apart, also come in handy and cost about $2.50.

✔ Utility knife. These knives generally have replaced the pocket knife for workshop use. They have razor-sharp blades that can be replaced and hand-fitting handles that make them easy to control. Price is about $1.

✔ Folding rule or steel tape. Whether measuring a floor for a rug or windows for drapes, the householder will frequently need something bigger than a yardstick. Steel tapes retract into compact cases. An eight-foot tape costs about $1.50. Tapes also come in 10-, 12-, and 16-foot lengths. Folding or zig-zag rules normally are six feet long and cost about $1. Newer models have a blank side opposite the foot-and-inch markings so the user can make pencil marks on it when measuring.

✔ Plunger or force cup or "plumber's helper." This device is used to free clogged drains and toilets and costs about $1.75.

✔ Hand saw. Get a 24- or 26-inch long crosscut model with seven or eight "points," or teeth, to the inch. Desirable models cost $5 and up.

✔ Adjustable wrench. An 8- or 10-inch model is the best for general use. Price is about $3.50.

✔ Torpedo level. This type level is smaller and generally cheaper than ones used by construction workers. Get a nine-inch model for about $3.

✔ Drill. First comes the ratchet or push-type drill, useful for starting screw holes and, with screwdriver attachments, for driving screws. The cost is about $5. Then comes the versatile electric drill. Attachments convert it into a sander, a circular saw, a hole-cutting saw, a sharpener, a polisher, a screwdriver, or a wire brush. Variable-speed drills, which will accommodate bits with shafts of up to three-eighths of an inch in diameter, start at about $15.

✔ Try square. Shaped like the letter "L", the try square typically consists of a steel blade attached to a wooden handle at a 90-degree angle. The tool is used for drawing cutting guides on wood and for gauging the trueness of the ends and sides of milled lumber. Cost: About $3. The "rafter square" has two steel arms set at a 90-degree angle. One arm generally is 24 inches long; the other 16. It is used on larger pieces of lumber and is priced at about $4.

Steer away from cheap tools. They often fail to do the job or to give reasonable wear.

Start with a bare minimum of tools, adding new ones only as they are needed.

Avoid low-cost "combination" or "wonder" tools touted as doing a variety of different jobs. Often they fail to perform even a single function well.

Rent and try out a power tool before buying. The device may prove less practical than it seemed.

KITCHEN CLEANSING AGENTS, such as drain cleaners, scouring powders, and dishwasher detergents, can damage garbage-disposal units and sink drains if they are not rinsed adequately. These compounds often are corrosive, particularly when left in contact with aluminum fittings. Housewives should look for rusting and pitting on the bottoms of disposal units and on elbow drains under sinks as warning signs of corrosion and leaks. To prevent deterioration, sinks should be flushed thoroughly after being scoured. Disposal units should be turned on during flushing to help remove caustic deposits in the units and in drains.

Danger! Low Voltage

LOW house voltage can damage electric motors in appliances. Although low voltage is not a common problem in today's homes, it is a characteristic of some older buildings and neighborhoods with inadequate wiring and overburdened circuits. The problem is aggravated if the local power company reduces its voltage output to conserve electricity during peak consumption periods.

More and more electric-power companies, especially in the populous Northeast, are being forced to reduce their voltage outputs during heat waves in summer, when air conditioners and other equipment are exerting their greatest demands on power sources. This may also happen during the winter; some cold snaps require more electricity for heating than power companies are equipped to supply.

Voltage can be regarded as the pressure that forces electricity into homes and through appliances. Most appliances are designed to operate at about 115 volts, although they have tolerances that allow them to operate normally at perhaps 10 per cent above or below that level. The standard voltage in some areas may be 110 or 120 volts instead of 115. Some large appliances, such as electric stoves and clothes dryers, operate at more than 200 volts and require special, high-voltage circuits. This higher voltage usually is from 220 to 240 volts.

Below-normal voltage usually does no harm to electrically operated housewares that are not motor driven.

But light bulbs will burn more dimly, television pictures will shrink, and irons, toasters, and electric ovens will heat up more slowly. This is because the lower voltage is forcing less electricity through the appliances.

Serious problems may arise, however, with motors in appliances, especially motors that are put under full load at the moment they are turned on. This happens to motors in refrigerators, air conditioners, and washers. It may take several times the flow of electricity necessary for normal operation to get such motors started. Normally this extraordinary starting flow lasts less than a second.

When voltage is low, it may not push enough electricity through a motor to start it turning. However, what is being pushed through is still much more than the usual flow. And this abnormal flow persists because the motor will not turn. This can overheat wiring, create short circuits, and cause the motor to "burn out." Repair or replacement of a motor often is expensive. And sometimes an overheated motor can damage other parts of an appliance.

Usually, however, the motors will not burn out, even if the local electric company reduces its voltage. If the lower voltage is within the operating tolerance of the motor, nothing out of the ordinary will happen at all. But if the voltage drops below the acceptable level, a fuse will blow out or a circuit breaker will open—perhaps in the appliance itself—before damage is done to the motor.

A person who lives in an area where peak summer and winter power demands may force an electric company to reduce voltage should be particularly alert for signs of low voltage under normal circumstances. If he has such a problem, there is more likelihood that motors will be damaged if his utility further reduces power during a shortage.

Some indications of low voltage may suggest inadequacies in either home wiring or in the utility company's power lines. Indications of this type include lights that dim when an appliance like an electric frying pan is switched on or appliances that seem to run slowly or strain to get started. If, however, your lights dim when a neighbor starts an appliance in his home, it is an almost sure sign that the trouble is in the utility-company supply lines.

If you suspect inadequate house wiring or a substandard utility power line, call your utility company. Their engineers usually can pinpoint the trouble by some simple tests. Many companies make some such checks at no cost.

New wiring may be called for if the system in your home is clearly inadequate to handle your appliances. Sometimes, though, you may be able to take some steps to minimize problems caused by inadequate house wiring. Most homes have several circuits, each with its own fuse or circuit breaker. An overload on a particular circuit can sometimes be eliminated if there is an underused circuit to which an appliance can be shifted.

Fuses or circuit breakers are the safety valves of electrical circuits. If they are of the proper size, which is usually indicated on the box or cabinet housing them, they will burn out or trip if a circuit becomes overloaded. This minimizes the possibility of damaged motors or fires from overheated wiring.

There is often a temptation to put fuses or circuit breakers of larger size on troublesome circuits rather than repeatedly replace fuses or reset tripped breakers. To do this, however, creates a fire hazard and increases the chance of motor damage.

If your power company announces a voltage reduction during a period of peak demand, keep an eye on motor-driven appliances, particularly those that are turned on and off automatically by timers or thermostats. If they don't appear to be operating properly, switch them off. If an appliance is urgently needed, you may be able to get enough electricity through the circuit to make it run normally by switching off all other lights and electrical devices on its circuit.

ALL FLASHLIGHT BATTERIES cannot be as readily recharged as some advertisements for chargers indicate. The common or primary cell does not lend itself to effective recharging as it is used in most homes, says the Council of Better Business Bureaus, Inc. Some users of large quantities of primary cells, who have test equipment not found in the ordinary home, are able to recharge the batteries economically. But the home user, who wants to reuse batteries probably would do better to buy more expensive batteries classified as secondary, which are designed to be recharged.

ELEVEN LOW-COST HOMES have been developed by the U.S. Forest Service. Though intended primarily for rural homes, the plans may be useful to persons contemplating a second vacation home. The designs emphasize simplicity and economical materials. Cost of detailed plans ranges from $1 to $1.70. However, sketches of the houses and order forms for plans are available for 25 cents from the Government Printing Office, Sales Planning Section, Box 1533, Washington, D.C. 20013. Ask for the order form for "Designs for Low-Cost Wood Homes."

Egg Grades

THE strain on the family food budget sometimes can be eased a little by care in shopping for eggs.

A housewife who knows the significance of Federal or state egg grading can avoid buying high-grade, more costly eggs when eggs of a lower grade will meet her particular needs about as well.

Not all egg cartons bear the seal showing the U.S. Department of Agriculture (USDA) grade and size. Only those egg producers who request grading and who pay a fee can display the seal. But states have their own grade and size regulations, which correspond closely to the Federal standards.

Eggs judged by USDA-licensed graders are assigned four grades: AA or fresh fancy, A, B, and C. The grades have nothing to do with nutrition but tell how stiff or viscous the eggs are and hence how they can best be used.

In a process called "candling," eggs are passed before a light and graders judge their contents. The stiffer and more compact the yolk and the white, the higher the grade. Grade-AA eggs are quite stiff and make good poached or fried eggs. Grade-A eggs are a little runnier but they are almost as satisfactory for the same dishes as Grade-AA eggs. Grade-B eggs are best for scrambled eggs and as ingredients in complex dishes. Grade-C eggs are used only in processing commercial egg products.

In addition to the letter grade for stiffness or viscosity, egg cartons also bear a grade indication for size. This is determined by the weight of a dozen eggs. The grades: jumbo, at least 30 ounces; extra large, 27 ounces; large, 24 ounces; medium, 21 ounces, small, 18 ounces; and peewee, 15 ounces. Extra large, large, and medium are the sizes most frequently found in markets.

If eggs are to be mixed with each other for, say, scrambled eggs or in a cake, buy the size egg that costs the least per ounce. If the size of an individual egg is important, some nutritionists have a rule-of-thumb that the larger size is a good buy if the per-dozen price is not more than 6 cents more than for the smaller size.

The nutritive value of eggs of a given size once varied from season to season because of variations in the feed given hens. Now, however, poultry diets have been standardized, and size has the only major effect on nutrition.

The color of the shell of an egg has nothing to do with its nutritive value. In some sections of the country, however, brown eggs are favored over white eggs or vice versa. Sometimes this causes a small price increase on eggs of the more popular color, and the thrifty housewife can save by buying eggs of the other color.

Age and heat reduce egg firmness. Eggs refrigerated at 32 to 50 degrees will retain their stiffness for several weeks but rapidly get thinner at higher temperatures. The USDA estimates that eggs will lose more quality in one day without refrigeration than they will in a week with refrigeration.

Quality loss is due to the porosity of egg shells. Carbon dioxide seeps out of the pores, especially if the pores are enlarged by heat. Carbon dioxide loss brings about a chemical change in egg protein that makes it runnier. A runny egg will look larger in a frying pan than a stiff egg of the same weight.

The egg's porous shell poses other problems for the consumer. Odors will seep into the egg if it is kept next to strong-smelling foods in a refrigerator. Dirt on the shell also will seep in so it is advisable to avoid eggs smudged with dirt.

Determining the freshness of eggs is made easier in some localities where cartons are dated. However, it is not always clear what the dates mean. In some places they indicate when the eggs were laid and in others they show the date of delivery to the retail stores. If in doubt about the date on a carton, check with the store manager or with the local health department.

ATHLETES AND OTHERS working outdoors in the heat and humidity of late summer should replace water and body minerals lost through excessive sweating. Saline solution is better for this than salt tablets. To make a single salt tablet effective a person must drink three quarts of water. What's more, salt pills can irritate the stomach. To mix a proper saline solution add one tablespoon of salt to a gallon of water. Until athletes are conditioned to the heat and perspire less, they may need as much as three glasses of the solution per hour.

STUDDED SNOW TIRES can cause serious driving problems on wet or dry pavements and should be removed when the snow season has passed. The Department of Transportation says that imported tires with more than the needed number of steel studs seem to create the most danger. It urges several precautions: Limit the number of studs in tires to an absolute maximum of 150 (100 is better and suitable for snow conditions in most of the nation). Have studs spaced evenly around the tire's circumference.

A TAX DEDUCTION for the cost of installing downstairs bathroom facilities for a taxpayer who could not climb stairs because of a heart condition has been allowed by the Internal Revenue Service. The IRS says that such an expense is deductible "if it has as its primary purpose the medical care of the taxpayer."

Protecting Against 'Locusts'

THE vandalism of thousands of unusual teenagers on their first fling causes dismay in many well-ordered neighborhoods nearly every year. The teenagers are 17-year cicadas, often erroneously called locusts.

The insects are born in trees, then spend nearly all their lives underground. There are 17 broods of these cicadas. Every year or so one or more broods, after 17 years underground, makes a mass migration back into the trees to deposit eggs. Brood X, which appeared last in 1970, is the largest of the broods. There are also 13 broods of 13-year cicadas.

The egg laying causes the vandalism. To fasten their eggs securely, cicadas carve tiny slits into branches with two sawlike appendages called ovipositors. The carving can kill or severely damage trees or shrubs.

Although they have been known to settle for any available type of wood, cicadas prefer to leave their broods in fruit trees, shrubs, and hardwoods like hickory and oak. Gummy softwoods like pines are less suitable.

Two simple methods are available for protecting small trees and shrubs. The homeowner who discovers cicadas while they are still on the ground can cover shrubs or small trees with cheesecloth, fastening it tightly at the trunks. This should be kept on for about a month. Spraying with an insecticide called carbaryl, often sold as "Sevin," is also effective. Three to five sprayings at one-week intervals usually does the trick. Avoid spraying the insecticide, which is harmful to honey bees, around flowering plants. Early morning or late afternoon, when the bees aren't likely to be around, is a good time for spraying.

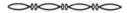

COPENHAGEN, DENMARK, has become so popular with tourists that hotel rooms are hard to find, prices are going up, and the traditional Danish courtesy and good humor sometimes wear thin. Scores of smaller cities in Denmark, many within a hour's driving time of Copenhagen, remain relatively untarnished by too much popularity.

One such charming little town is Roskilde, located about 20 miles west of Copenhagen. Drop by the *Vikingeskibshallen,* a handsome museum where Eleventh Century Viking ships are displayed. The building is located on the shores of the fiord in which the ships were found.

Roskilde Cathedral, built in the 1170s, is astonishingly clean and well preserved. It houses the remains of many Danish kings and is the successor to a church built in 960 by Harald Bluetooth, the country's first Christian king.

Caution: Visitors traveling to or in Denmark by car should make advance reservations on the ferries tying the nation's islands together to avoid waits of as long as a day. Reservations may be made at Danish and Swedish state railway stations and at major stations of the federal railways of West Germany.

DRY-MARTINI fanciers can help solve the problem of lemon-peel supply for an occasional drink by tightly wrapping a lemon in a plastic sandwich bag after cutting off a slice of peel. The bag will keep the lemon in good shape and usable for more peel slicings far longer than simply returning it to the refrigerator unwrapped.

What Meat Grading

Doesn't Show

AT a meat counter in Wheaton, Md., a round steak labeled "prime" sells for $1.09 per pound. An almost identical "choice" round steak beside it goes for 10 cents a pound less. Despite the difference in grade and price, the "choice" steak may taste better than the "prime."

The reason isn't peculiar to meat at the Wheaton store; it is because of two factors—conformation and age—used in assigning Government quality grades to beef, which aren't entirely reliable.

Conformation, or the shape of a carcass, gives wholesalers and retailers a rough idea of how much lean meat they may get from a particular side of beef. But it doesn't tell consumers anything. Since conformation is one of six variables going into Government quality grades, beef from a thin animal will be downgraded even though the meat may look and taste as good as beef graded prime.

The Department of Agriculture, which administers the beef-grading program, presently is considering a suggestion from the American Meat Institute, an association of meat packers in Chicago, that conformation be removed from the list of factors used in determining quality grades.

The department has taken no formal stand on the matter, but if it proposes the grading change, a controversy is sure to ensue. As early as 1962, the department discussed eliminating conformation but it backed off a year later after a large segment of the beef industry protested.

Breeders of purebred cattle objected because they feared the proposal would raise the quality grades of non-purebred and dairy cattle, which often fail to measure up well on conformation.

The meat from purebred cattle isn't necessarily more palatable, although the odds are favorable that purebred cattle will yield meat that tastes good. Purebreds are desirable simply because their genetic histories are known and it's fairly easy to predict that they will have certain desirable qualities.

One Agriculture Department official says the department dropped the conformation proposal because it feared powerful cattlemen opposed to the change would pressure legislators to pare down the department's budget. But John C. Pierce, who heads the department's livestock division, contends the idea was abandoned because "the grades are not going to be useful to anyone if industry won't use them."

Mr. Pierce's observation points up that meat is graded for quality only if the meat packer elects to pay over $10 an hour for a Federal grader to judge his meat. (All beef in interstate commerce, however, must meet separate Federal standards for wholesomeness and sanitation.)

The optional quality inspection is made while beef is suspended in a refrigerated room after slaughter. A plant employe slits each carcass between the 12th and 13th ribs, exposing a rib muscle. A Federal grader comes along about 30 minutes later to examine the exposed meat for color, texture, firmness, and the amount of fat "marbled" or swirled through it. He also considers the age of each animal before it was killed. And he sizes up carcass conformation in a glance.

Poor conformation lowers the quality grade from "prime" or "choice" to "choice" or "good" on only 5 per cent of the graded beef, according to Mr. Pierce. But how much beef is kept from meat counters because conformation prevents it from being graded "good" or better isn't known. Such low-priority beef commonly is sold to hospitals and schools, or put into processed foods such as bologna.

Even if conformation were removed from the quality grading, the age of a piece of beef would still present a problem in judging how it may taste.

Beef gradually grows more tender after it is slaughtered as the meat fibers that stiffened during *rigor mortis* "relax." Because the Government grades on beef include no date, "choice" beef served a week after slaughter may taste better than "prime" that is eaten within three days.

Most of the benefits of aging accrue in the first 10 days after slaughter, but beef continues to age even under refrigeration until it's cooked. Although the greater amount of beef sold is at least seven days old, a shopper may profit from buying his beef from a supermarket or grocery store that maintains a policy of aging its beef about two weeks to ensure its tenderness.

Ultimately, the best course of action in shopping for beef is to rely on personal judgment on whether a piece of meat looks good. In doing so, a customer may find meat graded lower than "prime" entirely satisfactory and thus may end up trimming the grocery bill.

Variable Annuities –
The Swingers

INFLATION has stirred considerable public interest in the variable annuity. It is one of many kinds of retirement-income plans.

It is, however, the only plan that makes it possible for retirees to receive fatter monthly checks as the cost of living goes up. It makes it *possible* for monthly payments to go up; it doesn't *guarantee* that they will.

Under the plan an insurance company takes premiums paid for variable annuities and invests them in common stocks, which vary in value from day to day. The variable annuity buyer thus acquires interest in a stock portfolio with a fluctuating value.

The buyer can benefit from this because when the agreed time comes for him to receive his variable-annuity payments, the portfolio may have gained value. Thus the buyer or annuitant gets more money. But stock values could drop in the interim between purchase of the plan and receipt of the first retirement-income check. Then the annuitant would get less money.

The variable annuity buyer, then, is gambling that stock values will go up and that the amount of income he eventually receives will bear a relation to inflated prices. Most insurance and regular annuity plans return income at a fixed rate.

Variable annuities are modifications of the well established basic annuity plans, which underlie most corporation pension plans. Understanding the variable annuity requires understanding the annuity.

The life-insurance policy pays if the policyholder dies; the annuity pays if the policyholder lives. The annuity buyer, seeking a guaranteed source of money after he has stopped working, pays the insurance company a premium. The company invests the individual's premium and, in turn, agrees to send the annuitant an agreed-on, monthly payment beginning on a stipulated, future date.

If the annuitant dies before the date of the first payment, his heirs may get nothing. If the annuitant lives for a long time after the date of the first payment, and actually runs through more than the entire amount of his premium, the company still must pay him.

Individuals can buy annuities in various ways. The simplest arrangement, often referred to as the single-premium immediate, calls for the annuitant to hand over a lump-sum payment to the insurance company, which usually begins making monthly payments the following month.

Relatively few persons have enough money to buy into a single-premium-immediate contract. It takes about $140 in principal for a person 65 years old to purchase $1 of monthly annuity payment. So if a 65-year-old retiree wanted to receive $100 a month for life starting next month, he would have to hand the insurer roughly $14,000.

More typically, persons buying annuities accumulate the needed principal by making monthly payments to an annuity account. They start the saving years before retirement.

They then may buy a level-premium deferred annuity. Under this agreement, the buyer declares that he intends to retire on a certain date and he figures out how much money he wants to receive each month after that date. The company calculates the amount of premium needed to make such an annuity possible. It breaks the total premium down into monthly payments.

Variable annuities are handled similarly. Some companies also allow buyers to make fluctuating payments into a variable annuity premium fund instead of the unvarying level payments.

The essential difference between the variable annuity and the regular annuity is that the regular annuity yields a fixed, predetermined payment; the variable annuity yields continually changing payments.

The variable-annuity purchaser builds up what insurance companies call accumulation units. They represent a portion of ownership in the insurance company's special, annuity-fund stock portfolio. The accumulation unit's value rises and falls daily just as a share of stock does. To compute its value on a given day the company divides the total number of units sold into the value of all the stock in the portfolio.

The variable-annuity buyer putting out $40 a month for his plan buys accumulation units at their current value. In March, for example, the buyer pays his $40. The unit's value then is $10 per unit: the buyer has four units credited to his account. In April, the buyer again pays his $40. The unit's value now has dropped to $5 per unit; so the buyer gets eight units. In May, the unit's value soars to $20; the buyer gets two units.

When the time arrives for the annuitant to begin receiving income, the company converts his total accumulation units into dollars on the basis of the value of the units at that time. It uses the money to buy annuity units. The annuity units are computed with a complicated mathematical formula. They are similar to accumulation units and also vary in value. Each month the company reckons the value of the annuity units owned by the buyer and sends him a check based on the current value of the annuity units credited to him.

All annuities have the advantage of providing some income. A variable annuity would return something each month even if the stocks backing it dropped sharply in value.

Variable annuities now offer tax advantages to self-employed persons and employes of public schools, colleges, and universities, and designated nonprofit organizations. Within certain limits, these persons can exclude payments for annuities from taxable income. They must pay taxes on the payments received after retirement, but by then the annuitant generally is in a lower tax bracket and thus pays less tax.

Variable-annuity acquisition charges, the fees charged by a company for commissions, processing, and the like are charged just once at the time of purchase. This could mean a saving to those who might otherwise buy mutual funds or other equity holdings to be converted later into annuities. Conversion generally entails paying fees at least twice, once when the equity is bought or sold and again when the annuity is purchased.

Choosing among available variable plans is hard for the layman. Acquisition and service charges levied by insurance companies are difficult to determine and compare. The brochures handed out by variable-annuity salesmen may mystify more than they inform, but the inflation-fighting feature of variable annuities makes them worth considering.

No-Load Mutual Funds

PITY the small investor. His investment decisions are usually wrong, according to Wall Street folklore. He has become *persona non grata* in many brokerage houses because he does not generate big sales commissions. The Government has stopped letting him buy high-yield Treasury bills, except in amounts of $10,000 or more. The fees he pays for investing in securities have been increased. Yet inflation keeps eroding his savings.

These factors collectively may help explain the sharp growth of a small segment of the mutual-fund industry—the no-load mutual funds. "It'll be nothing but no-loads for me from now on," a stock investor fumed recently on hearing about the hike in brokerage charges.

No-loads are investment trusts that make no sales or redemption charge. They offer a way for the investor with the economy-size bankroll to get a piece of the stock-market action at little cost—and with professional portfolio management in the bargain. From a performance standpoint, many no-loads compare favorably with load funds.

Most mutual funds impose a sales charge, or "load," amounting to between $85 and $93 of every $1,000 invested. This pays for salesman's commission, plus costs of advertising and distribution. The mutual-fund industry owes much of its impressive growth to aggressive salesmanship.

No-load funds employ no salesmen, so there is no load charge. Of every dollar invested, practically all goes into fund shares, which are purchased directly from the company, usually by mail. Thus, no-loads represent a kind of "do-it-yourself" investing; prospective customers usually must contact the funds on their own, write for information, and make their own evaluation of how well a particular fund meets their personal investment objectives.

The no-loads' big selling point, of course, is the lack of a sales charge, and they emphasize this in their promotional material. But because no salesmen are out beating the bushes for customers, relatively few people know they exist. As more and more investors discover them, no-loads have become one of the fastest growing segments of the securities business.

Since 1965 the number of no-load shareholders has soared to more than 832,000, from about 257,000, says Irving L. Straus Associates, Inc., a New York public-relations company that represents one of the no-loads. Assets of these funds have risen to $3.1 billion from $1.5 billion during that period. The no-load funds now make up 7 percent of the mutual-fund industry.

Precise comparisons with load-fund growth are not available. However, the Investment Company Institute (ICI) reports that assets of its members climbed to $48.3 billion at the end of January 1970 from $35.2 billion in 1965. The number of shareholders rose to 5,600,000 from 3,500,000. The institute is composed of companies operating about 300 funds that account for approximately 90 per cent of all mutual-fund assets, load and no-load.

Aside from the self-service feature and lack of sales charges, no-loads are similar to load funds. Both types are investment companies, or trusts, which sell shares to the public and invest the proceeds in a diversified portfolio of securities. Both offer professional money management to investors who may not have the time or expertise to manage their own investments. This service isn't free, though. Investors in both load and no-load funds pay a managerial fee; it generally runs about 0.5 per cent or less of the fund's total assets.

The two types of funds offer various special features, such as income-reinvestment plans, retirement plans, and vehicles for investing on a periodic-payment basis. Like load funds, different loads aim for different investment objectives, such as growth of capital, regular income, or a combination of both. Funds that try for the latter are called "balanced" funds.

No-load funds have been around at least since the 1920s, but most of their growth has come recently.

Invariably, investment advisers emphasize that no one should select a mutual fund solely because it does not make a sales charge. Performances of no-load funds vary widely, as do those of load funds. "When trying to determine which funds give you your dollars' worth, the fact is that some no-load funds are a bargain—and some are 'very expensive,'" notes FundScope, a monthly magazine which analyzes and rates mutual funds in depth. "The fact is, there is no correlation between results, on the one hand, and the load (or absence of load) on the other. There is just no relationship between what a fund 'does' and what it charges you to do."

One study indicated that, as a group, no-load funds have performed about as well as load funds over the past several years, but that no-load investors did somewhat better in terms of actual net gains because of the absence of a sales charge.

Here are some prime sources of information about no-load funds:

✔ A list of more than 100 no-loads can be obtained free by writing to DRI Research, Ltd., an affiliate of Irving L. Straus Associates, Inc., 375 Park Ave., New York, N.Y. 10022. Names and addresses are provided, along with the founding date, investment objectives, and total net assets of each fund.

✔ General information about no-loads and basic data for about 42 member funds can be obtained from the No-Load Mutual Fund Association, Suite 3401, 375 Park Ave., New York, N.Y., 10022.

✔ If a fund you're interested in does not appear on that list, try the Investment Company Institute, 1775 K Street NW., Washington, D.C. 20006.

✔ To get detailed information about an individual fund, write or telephone the fund itself. Ask for a prospectus, the latest financial statement, and any other literature available. From this material you can find out who manages the fund, how it has performed in the past, what securities it holds, its aims and objectives, and details about special features or restrictions.

✔ Comparative Data on many funds, load and no-load, can be found in *Investment Companies, 1971,* published by Arthur Wiesenberger Services Division of Nuveen Corp., 61 Broadway, New York, N.Y. 10004. This is an annual reference work that sells for $45 but is available in many public libraries, along with other publications on investing.

Reports on the performance of more than 440 funds, load and no-load, are issued weekly by the Arthur Lipper Corp. of New York. These are not publicly circulated, but copies are usually available from brokerage offices.

Daily quotations of mutual-fund prices can be

found in the financial sections of many metropolitan newspapers and in publications such as The Wall Street Journal. Barron's National Business and Financial Weekly, 30 Broad St., New York, N.Y. 10004, also provides quarterly reports on funds plus a review of developments in the industry.

DISCOUNT "CLUB" offers of recent-model used cars at far below the normal used-car market prices should be viewed with great caution, warns the Council of Better Business Bureaus, Inc. Many of these clubs do not reveal until after a substantial deposit has been collected that the vehicles involved have been used as taxis or in other high-mileage, high-wear use. The purchaser usually has no opportunity to see the vehicle until he arrives at a designated place to take delivery. The purchase of any used car involves risk by the buyer, even when he has the opportunity to inspect and drive the vehicle before committing himself to buy. Sight-unseen commitments invite disappointment.

OLDER PERSONS can save money on travel and accommodations in Switzerland with a special voucher costing $12.65 a year. Available at main Swiss railroad stations to men over 64 and women over 62, the voucher is good for year-around unlimited travel at half fare on Swiss trains, boats, and postal motor coaches. It is also good for reductions in the off travel season of from 10 to 20 per cent of the regular room rates at 500 hotels. A folder listing the hotels participating in the Season for Seniors program is available from the Swiss National Tourist Office, 608 Fifth Ave., New York City 10020, or 661 Market St., San Francisco 94105.

BUBBLES MEAN TROUBLES when they show up while you are varnishing. They are caused by the bristles in the paint brush. To minimize the problem, apply varnish with smooth even strokes, brushing as little as possible. If bubbles do appear, light brushing should rid them.

The Small Investor
& Real Estate

REAL estate has long held a strong fascination for the small investor. But only recently has he had much of a choice of ways to enter this complex field at moderate cost through what are called real-estate mutual funds, real-estate investment trusts, or just REITs.

Inflation stimulated interest in REITs; real estate has traditionally been used to hedge against erosion of the dollar's value. But the trusts' recent performance has been an even bigger attraction. As a group, REITs have done better than the stock-market averages for several years. Many of the trusts also pay above-average yields of between 7 per cent and 10 per cent annually.

How the trusts will fare in the future is anybody's guess. But a number of analysts believe that the outlook for them is promising. Pent-up housing demand, major building programs in urban areas, and development of new transportation systems are expected to offer plenty of outlets for investment of REIT funds. "I'm bullish," declares Kenneth Campbell, publisher of Realty Trust Review, a newsletter on real-estate securities. "Over the long term, REITs should be very attractive."

REITs are similar to mutual funds in that they sell shares to investors and invest the proceeds, sharing any gains or losses with the shareholder. But whereas mutual funds usually put their money in securities, REITs invest in real property, or make real-estate loans. Shares of the major REITs are traded on stock exchanges or the over-the-counter market, and their value therefore is influenced to an extent by stock-market fluctuations.

There are close to 90 publicly held trusts with an aggregate value of about $4 billion, and several new ones are being formed. The National Association of Real Estate Investment Trusts, a trade group based in New Haven, Conn., counts 177 trusts in all, including private offerings. At the beginning of 1969 there were some 20 publicly held REITs with assets totaling $600,000,000.

The trusts took a drubbing in the early 1960s because of a stock-market slump and the collapse of several real-estate empires. But the better-managed REITs survived.

Realty trusts fall mainly into two categories: equity trusts, which own property and get their income from rents collected by professional property managers, and mortgage trusts, which derive most of their income from property loans. There are two mortgage-trust subdivisions: those that make long-term loans and those that lend chiefly for the short term. REITs aren't permitted to directly manage their own properties, and they can't develop land or buy real estate for quick resale.

A performance index maintained by Paine, Webber, Jackson & Curtis, a leading brokerage house, shows that mortgage trusts have outperformed both equity trusts and the Dow Jones index of blue-chip industrial stocks over the past four years.

Following is a sampler of both equity and mortgage trusts, showing for each the date of issue, adjusted price of a share in the first offering, the share price on April

12, 1971, and the percentage yield based on the April 12 price:

Equity Trusts—U.S. Realty Investments, June 24, 1961, $10, $20, 7.5 per cent; National Realty Investors, March 14, 1962, $15, $12, 6.6 per cent; Franklin Realty, April 6, 1962, $12.50, $10.38, 7.3 per cent; Realty Income Trust, June 26, 1969, $16.50, $17, 5.8 per cent; and Hubbard Real Estate Investments, Nov. 6, 1969, $25, $24.50, 5.8 per cent.

Mortgage Trusts—Continental Mortgage Investors, March 22, 1962, $2.50, $23.88, 4.3 per cent; First Mortgage Investors, Sept. 22, 1961, $9.38, $32.88, 6.6 per cent; Guardian Mortgage Investors, March 4, 1969, $25, $36.50, 8.1 per cent; Great American Mortgage Investors, July 29, 1969, $21, $27.12, 5.9 per cent; and Mortgage Trust of America, Nov. 6, 1969, $20, $25.62, 7.8 per cent.

REITs come in a bewildering variety; picking one that fits particular investment objectives can be difficult for the average investor. Knowing something about the intricacies of real-estate financing may help, but knowledgeable investment advisers also place great stress on a trust's past performance, its investment philosophy, the quality of the sponsoring company.

Probably the most detailed information about a trust's management, resources, operations, strategy, and risk factors can be obtained from the prospectus, or offering statement, which all companies selling securities to the public must provide. Price fluctuations of listed REIT shares can be obtained from many newspapers and financial publications, such as The Wall Street Journal. Occasionally, such publications offer specific buy and sell recommendations. Mr. Campbell's newsletter provides detailed performance comparisons, comments, and recommendations, but the price is steep—

$84 a year. The publication is available from Audit Investment Research, Inc., 230 Park Ave., New York City 10017.

Names and addresses of REITs can usually be obtained from a stockbroker. The National Association of Real Estate Investment Trusts publishes an annual handbook that profiles 52 trusts; it can be obtained for $17.50 from the organization at 900 Chapel St., New Haven, Conn. 06510.

Equity and mortgage trusts use quite different investment approaches, although some REITs combine some features of each. Equity trusts buy property—everything from shopping centers, apartments, and office buildings to oil wells and vacant land. Shareholders can benefit both from income these holdings produce and from appreciation in their value. As properties grow older, the trusts claim depreciation tax deductions.

Among the larger equity trusts are U.S. Realty Investments, Hubbard Real Estate Investments, Pennsylvania Real Estate Investment Trust, and Real Estate Investment Trust of America.

Mortgage trusts finance numerous types of real-estate operations and distribute the interest and fees to shareholders. Though they can't claim depreciation allowances on property they don't own, mortgage trusts can generate higher profits through "leverage." That means that they can borrow relatively large amounts of cash on a limited amount of equity and put the money to work. By borrowing from banks at, say, 7½ per cent interest and putting the money into short-term construction and development loans at 9 to 11 per cent, a trust can make a substantial profit.

Some of the better-known mortgage trusts are Chase Manhattan Mortgage and Realty Trust, Continental Mortgage Investors, General Mortgage Investors, Mortgage Trust of America, and B. F. Saul Real Estate Investment Trust.

Despite the recent gains, investing in REITs can be hazardous. Some analysts contend that trust operations are beyond the comprehension of many investors, and even some investment specialists have trouble evaluating them. "The phenomenon of the real-estate investment trust is still new enough that most investors, and many securities analysts, are not yet very familiar with it," asserts a West Coast observer.

OUTDOOR BARBECUE GRILLS will last longer if their bowls are kept clean and dry and the grill is periodically painted with one of the paints designed for application to articles subject to high temperatures. The paints, designed to resist heat of from 800 to 1,000 degrees, are available both in regular paint form and in spray cans.

KEEP TALCUM POWDER out of the reach of toddlers. The British Medical Journal reports that a number of one- and two-year-olds have suffocated after spilling powder in large quantities and inhaling it. Excessive quantities of powder forms a sticky, inflammatory substance when inhaled, which can block air passages and damage the lungs.

PACKAGES: If you are weary of the slow speed and high cost of sending packages by parcel post or REA, check into the availability of United Parcel Service (UPS) in your area. UPS frequently is faster and cheaper than either the mails or REA surface shipments.

TENT CAMPERS can use empty beer or soft-drink cans to reduce or eliminate the problem of tent poles sinking into sand or soft soil. Stand each pole in a can from which one end has been cut out. The technique is particularly useful for beach camping.

Second Homes –
A Growing Trend

BE it ever so humble—or imaginative, imposing, or opulent—there's no place like a second home.

So many Americans are seeking vacation or leisure homes these days that construction of second homes is booming even though construction of primary housing is in a severe slump.

The second-home boom touches much of the nation. In Virginia's Blue Ridge Mountains, for example, model-home displays speckle the sides of highways leading from the Baltimore and Washington, D.C., metropolitan areas. Scattered among the lake-dotted hills and valleys are thousands of shelters of every description. For less than $10,000, a refugee from the nerve-jangling strains of urban living can obtain a comfortable hideaway, complete with plumbing, tranquility, and vistas.

Sundance Leisure Homes of Paris, Va., put up a model of a $6,995 chalet alongside U.S. Highway 50. Three weeks later, said partners John Weir and John Wright, 15 passing motorists had stopped, looked, and signed contracts.

The Jim Walter Corp. of Tampa, Fla., which claims to be the nation's largest producer of recreation housing, reports that its sales in this category rose to $61,-000,000 in the fiscal year ended Aug. 31, 1970, from $55,000,000 in the comparable 1969 period.

About 90,000 second homes were built throughout the nation in 1970, 150 per cent more than in 1960, estimates the National Association of Home Builders. By 1975, the annual total will reach 150,000, the association predicts.

A survey by the Commerce and Agriculture departments shows that, as of April 1967, some 1,700,000 U.S. families owned second homes.

The industry has enjoyed steady growth since the 1940s, when the number of starts averaged 20,000 a year. But a sharp spurt came with the rising affluence of the 1960s. Chief reasons for the popularity of second homes: a growing interest in nature and wilderness areas; aversion to urban living; increased leisure time; and improved highways.

"Coming out here from the city is like escaping to paradise from a chain gang," exclaims George G. Clark, a Baltimore civil engineer and owner of a cozy cabin with a sweeping view of the Shenandoah Valley.

Second homes come in many varieties, with prices ranging into six figures. The Government survey, however, places the median value at $7,800. A handyman on a budget can get by for less than that. Vacation-home lots can be purchased in many places for $2,000 or less, and some cottages with unfinished interiors are available for less than that. Northern Counties Lumber, Inc., of Upperville, Va., offers a 20- by 24-foot shell cottage for $2,400, erected on any site within 50 miles of its plant. For $200 more, the structure can be partitioned off into five rooms.

Jim Walter's best seller is its highest-priced model —a piling-supported, 20x32-foot dwelling with a deck. It costs just under $6,000 as a shell and $8,700 complete, including plumbing.

Richard L. Ragatz, who made a study of recreational housing for a doctoral dissertation at Cornell University, estimates that costs of a second home now average about $8,000. The most popular design is the A-frame, which accounted for 34 per cent of the construction studied. Among other types, cabins made up 31 per cent and chalets and ranchers 10 per cent each.

Vacation homes, not surprisingly, tend to be clustered around lakes, seashore areas, golf courses, or rivers and streams. Despite the mushrooming of planned resorts in recent years, most such dwellings are on scattered individual lots or acreage.

The Washington-based American Land Developers Association estimates that some 200 companies around the country now build or manufacture recreational housing. New or improved materials and construction techniques, such as prefabrication, premanufacturing, and prehanging of doors and windows helps keep costs down.

If a customer owns his lot outright, a builder often will finance the entire cost of the structure. Jim Walter offers fairly typical terms: 12 years at 11.5 per cent annual interest.

The second-home market has spawned thousands of promotional subdivisions, many of them sucker traps. But some developments have grown in value and attractiveness. In this area, Shenandoah Farms, for example, was a 6,000-acre expanse of wilderness a decade ago. Today it is a community of middle-income families in which $6,000,000 has been invested.

Of the 2,000 persons who have bought lots, some 400 have built secluded retreats among high mountain slopes or along the winding Shenandoah River. Prices of half-acre lots have risen to $2,800 from $1,000.

Along with clean air, majestic vistas, and serenity, residents can avail themselves of such activities as swimming in a heated pool, fishing, hiking, or horseback riding.

John D. Flynn, Jr., co-founder of the project, credits its success in part to association with a building concern that operates year-round on the premises. "If lot buyers don't build, the land just sits there," notes Gayle T. Dorman, vice president of Mountain View Homes, Inc. "Without a builder around, people don't know where to turn. They find themselves in all kinds of difficulties."

Mr. Dorman, 34, foresaw the explosive demand for recreational housing several years ago, and switched from primary to second-home construction. "The first couple of years were pretty rough," he relates. In 1963 his company put up just 12 houses. This year the total will run about 60, and with the demand continually increasing as a result of lot sales, Mr. Dorman looks for the number to increase at an annual rate of 10 per cent to 15 per cent.

Mr. Dorman and Mr. Flynn will go out of their way to keep customers happy even after they've sold property to them. In 1968, when the area was hit with power failure during a hard freeze, the two rode around on a tractor for two days draining water from 125 homes so that the pipes wouldn't freeze and burst.

EASE THE STRAIN of hefting weighty loads such as small trees and shrubs or sacks of peat moss and cement by rolling the sack onto a plastic sheet and using the sheet as a skid. The plastic lessens friction on grass and leaves. And when solidly implanted posts and stumps must be raised, try fixing a looped chain to the object, then to a bumper jack. The pumping action on the jack, which can lift an automobile, generally can oust a stuck fence post.

Cameras and Computers
Aid Duffers

BUYING golf clubs is about as exact an exercise as divining water. At least it was until the Swing Recorder came along. This camera-computer combination apparently has provided objective data about clubs, and seems to have taken some of the vagueness out of buying these expensive playthings—clubs range in price from $45 to more than $450 a set.

The Swing Recorder is what its inventor, Emanuel James Betinis, golfer, mathematician, and computer analyst, calls a "photo-analytic, semi-analog computer." It photographs a golfer at a specific point in his swing, determines his maximum hitting potential, and comes up with club specifications that help him reach his potential.

Part of the complex gadget's operation calls for superimposing graphs over the photo. Figures read from the graphs serve as a key to specifications of the ideal club.

There are nine widely scattered Swing Recorders at the moment, most in the shops of golf professionals. Owners insist the computers work well, and that they can help all but the rawest tyro pick clubs that will help his game.

Some 80 per cent of the touring professionals have consulted the computer to check their swings. Some have bought new clubs after viewing the results.

Though the computers are currently accessible to few of the nation's 11,000,000 golfers, the general information they have churned up may help others. And from the computers' analyses come these tips:

The "feel" of the club, generally touted as the most important factor in club selection, is a practically useless guide.

"Swing weight," which refers to the distribution of weight between the club's various parts, is relatively unimportant. Swing weights have been coded and stamped on clubs. Clubs with low swing weights (L, DO, D1, D2) have least weight in the club head, the part that hits the ball. Higher swing weights are designated (D4, D5, D6). Custom-made clubs may have even higher swing weights.

"Hard hitters" normally are advised to buy clubs with high swing weights. Yet analysis shows that even hard hitters tend to lose control of a club if the head is too heavy. The vast majority of golfers should stick with moderately weighted clubs.

Flexibility of the club shaft, which also is coded and which varies according to the type of metal used, is the single most important factor in helping or hurting a golfer's game.

Flexibility varies from extra stiff to whippy. Carbon steel yields the stiffest clubs, a new steel-alloy giving medium stiffness, and aluminum generally providing the whippy shafts.

It is commonly assumed that hard hitters need stiff clubs. The machine indicates that few golfers can reach their potential using stiff clubs; flexible shafts, often aluminum, which many veteran golfers disdain, seem to suit most golfers best.

"Matched sets" of clubs, the more expensive ones that allegedly eliminate all but essential differences in the 14 kinds of clubs in a set, often vary noticeably in ways they should not.

Clubs in a set may differ in over-all weight and in shaft stiffness, and may have errors in relative degree of loft. Loft is the degree of slant of the clubhead's "face," the part of the club that actually swats the ball.

Choice of club length isn't the simple decision it commonly is believed to be. To a certain extent it is true that the tall need long clubs and the short need short ones. Yet the computer reveals that many persons who follow this axiom may play with clubs of improper length.

More importantly the player must take into account the fit of the club as he addresses the ball.

Normally a player cannot judge for himself if his address is proper, so he cannot tell if the club length is proper. He must consult someone who can advise him. This is one of the strongest arguments for following standard advice to see a golf pro when buying clubs.

There is considerably less difference than advertised between brands of clubs in the same price group. Loft, weight, and the rest are similar.

The differences between higher and lower priced clubs by the same manufacturer are differences in the quality of the materials in hand grips and shafts.

Mr. Betinis has concluded that most cheap clubs do not perform as well as their better constructed counterparts probably because of the variations in shaft quality. Many golf pros concur.

Still, they do not urge the price-conscious buyer to purchase expensive clubs; they suggest purchasing used clubs, which often sell for less than half their original price and maintain trade-in value.

Cigars for All Tastes

THE suspicion that cigaret smoking increases chances of developing lung cancer has prompted many persons to change to cigars. Smokers who would rather switch than quit are faced with a bewildering array of cigars, which come in hundreds of sizes, shapes, shades, prices, and flavors.

You can buy them handmade or machine manufactured. Selecting a handmade cigar can be as involved as buying a precious bottle of wine, with the source and vintage of the tobacco held up to as much scrutiny as the grapes.

Or you can shun hundreds of years of tradition by picking out a mint-and-menthol-flavored cigar complete with plastic mouthpiece and an outer skin of homogenized tobacco that looks like brown wrapping paper. Smoking it provides little tobacco and feel.

Remember this if thinking of switching: Cigars are not loved by everyone; their smell and appearance can be offensive, especially to wives and working associates. Cigar ashes and butts tend to be conspicuous. Cigars can fill a small room or apartment with heavy smoke in a few moments. The smoke may cling to a smoker's clothes, foul his breath, and dull taste buds for long periods.

No one argues that cigars are healthy. The U.S. Public Health Service notes that nicotine in the smoke can enter the bloodstream through mouth and throat membranes. But what the nicotine does to the heart and other organs—or what the hot smoke does to the throat, mouth, and teeth—is not clear because the necessary tests have not been made. Public-health officials say only that the lack of inhalation frees a cigar smoker from some of the dangers of lung cancer and other respiratory disorders associated with cigarets.

The Cigar Institute of America, which represents most U.S. cigar manufacturers, tries to make choosing a cigar an easy process. "Pick out a cigar you're comfortable with," it says, "and pick one you can afford." For the smoker who wants to be a little more objective there are several other things to consider about cigars.

There are three parts to a cigar; the inside filler, the surrounding binder, and the outside tobacco wrapper. Most filler is tobacco blended from different sources. It may consist of nearly whole leaves or of shredded or chopped leaves. Both the binder and the wrapper may be either whole leaves or else sheets of tobacco pressed from pulverized leaves and stems.

Handmade cigars, which comprise less than 5 per cent of the American market, are made of all-leaf tobacco. They vary widely in quality and price. They can be bought for as little as 5 or 10 cents each, but the tobacco and handiwork may produce a harsh smoke. Better ones, most of them imported and available only in cigar specialty shops, cost up to $1.25 each. Whether they are worth the higher price is a matter of individual taste.

American machine-made cigars total more than eight billion annually and make up about 95 per cent of the market. They cost an average of 9 cents each; few are sold for more than 35 cents. One secret of the price advantage over handmade cigars is the processed or homogenized binder that almost all machine-made cigars have. Purists are quick to call such binders "paper," because they are made much the same way paper is from wood. Tobacco stems and leaves are pulverized, an adhesive or binding agent is added, the mixture is rolled into thin sheets. Parts of the tobacco leaf that once were unusable are now utilized and the binding can be made inexpensively by machine.

Manufacturers often use nontobacco additives in the binder and filler to make the cigar burn more uniformly, smoke milder, and taste better. By agreement with the Federal Trade Commission, which knows the additives but keeps them secret, these manufacturers must state on their labels: "These cigars are predominantly natural tobacco with nontobacco ingredients added."

But a smoker should not assume that he is avoiding a paperlike binder by choosing only cigars without such a label. If made by machine, they still are likely to have homogenized binders that look and behave very much like those with nontobacco additives. Both types of cigars may have a paper reinforcement around the tip of the cigar, underneath the wrapper, to keep the binder from being bitten through or literally melting in your mouth.

Experienced smokers say they can tell cigars with homogenized binders from their feel, appearance, and taste. Many don't like them, considering them artificial cigars. A novice probably would be unable to detect any differences among whole-leaf and the various manufactured binders.

Serious cigar smokers seldom agree on where the best tobacco comes from for filler, binder, and wrapper. Tobacco from certain parts of Cuba was highly favored until the United States placed an embargo on Cuban tobacco shipments after Castro took power. Cuban seeds have been transplanted in similar climates, but the resulting tobacco leaves have qualities of their own.

Machine-made cigars usually have shredded or chopped filler, which allows easier blending and handling. It gives a cigar a more uniform burn and more consistent taste, but also may make it burn faster and hotter unless the filler is packed tightly.

The color of outside wrappers ranges from light green to dark brown. This color has little bearing on how a cigar will smoke. The wrapper does add to the flavor, but the binder and filler are more important. The qualities of all three blend together to produce flavor. A cigar shop owner should be able to tell you the smoking qualities of a particular cigar, but in a drugstore you probably will be on your own.

The cigars that usually are considered best also burn most slowly. A 70-cent cigar made by hand with 1959 Cuban tobacco may take 1¼ hours to burn down from six to about three inches. The mint-menthol plastic-tip cigar burned 3½ inches in about 20 minutes.

Beginning cigar smokers may prefer plastic- or wooden-tipped cigars, as well as those with mint, menthol, rum, burgundy, and even cherry flavors. Cigaret-sized, filter-tipped cigars are available. They sometimes are very strong and their size may tempt the smoker to inhale; if he does, the health dangers are worse than from cigarets.

Fatter cigars tend to burn more slowly and coolly than thinner cigars of the same length, tobacco, and firmness. Air currents can make a cigar burn too fast, so many persons will not smoke them outdoors or in drafty automobiles.

If cigars are kept for more than a few days, they should be stored in a wooden or glass humidor that is relatively airtight and will retain the cigars' moisture.

Connoisseurs like to age cigars in humidors for as long as several years to improve taste. Dried-out cigars burn hot, although more smokers prefer them that way. A refrigerator makes a poor humidor; food odors are absorbed by tobacco.

A cigar will go out by itself if not puffed regularly. When you are through smoking it, you can avoid unnecessary odor by letting it go out instead of crushing it out.

A HOLE-IN-ONE is possibly the ultimate thrill for a golfer. But the thrill can be expensive: Traditionally the golfer is expected to buy drinks for everyone at the golf club.

An organization now offers bar-bill insurance plus a vacation for two for the hole-in-one maker. The Hole-in-One Club, 45 Rockefeller Plaza, New York City 10020, sells memberships for $10. More than 15,000 golfers have joined.

A member who gets a hole-in-one is covered for up to $200 in celebration expenses, then he can choose from among a variety of vacations to Hawaii, London, Paris, Rome, or Bermuda. Or he may elect a Caribbean cruise or a domestic trip of his choice. All transportation and accomodation costs are paid by the club.

To qualify, the golfer must score his ace during an 18-hole round on a course approved by the United States Golf Association. It must be attested by at least two witnesses and the club professional or a course official.

OLD MEDICINES should be discarded if they have changed color, separated, or become altered in any way. Many liquid medicines and pills lose or gain strength with age, and they can become either ineffective or dangerous. Medicines in damaged or defective containers, as well as those whose use has been forgotten, also should be thrown out. When discarding medicines, be sure they are put where children cannot find them.

Stripping the Mystery
From Stereos

HI-FI and stereo and their associated jargon, though not new, still mystify many. And now, confusing matters more, come advertisements for "omni-directional sound" and talk about "four-channel systems."

Hi-fi means high-fidelity reproduction of recordings; in a sense, it means quality. It refers to tape, phonograph, and radio equipment that comes closer than less expensive, electronic systems to reproducing music or other sounds as actually performed or spoken.

Stereo, short for stereophonic, describes sound recorded by microphones in two or more locations or the equipment to reproduce this sound, which may be recorded on double-track tapes or on two planes inside the single grooves of records. In a concert hall a person hears slightly different sounds from an orchestra in each ear and this separation gives depth to the music, stereo recording and playback systems attempt to duplicate this depth.

Stereo playback sets must have at least two loudspeakers. If the stereo is hi-fi and the speakers sit at least 6 to 10 feet apart, the sound reproduction should have dimension and heighten the illusion of hearing the sound as performed.

To increase the illusion, hi-fi equipment makers are now producing "four-channel" music—recording music, for instance, by placing microphones in at least four locations around the orchestra. They transfer the music to the equivalent of four-track tape and play it back on what amounts to two stereo systems.

An argument persists about the value of omni-directional, "360-degree," or "multi-directional" sound. The terms all refer to the acoustics of modified stereo speakers.

A single hi-fi stereo speaker really contains at least two speakers, a small "tweeter," for high tones, and a "woofer," for bass tones. In regular stereo speakers, tweeters and woofers face toward the cloth-covered front of rectangular cases. In a multi-directional speaker, the tweeter points toward the ceiling and at the point of a sound-deflecting cone. The woofer points toward the floor and at another cone. Woofer, tweeter, and cones sit in a cylindrical case. The arrangement supposedly encourages sound to pulse out equally in all directions.

Some hi-fi fans say the omni-directional speakers improve the sound; others contend they distort reproduction. Buyers should listen to regular and omni-directional speakers playing the same music to determine which they prefer.

Stereo systems, hi-fi and of lesser quantity, come in several forms:

Consoles. These all-in-one systems almost never contain hi-fi parts. Their speakers sit too close to produce the illusion of reality to any great extent. But they are cheaper than hi-fi stereo systems. They eliminate all need for assembling.

Portables. Mostly produced by console makers, they have movable speakers that can be spaced properly. They take up less room than consoles, and they are relatively cheap. Few contain hi-fi parts, and their sound suffers by comparison with hi-fi stereo.

Compacts. These hi-fi stereo sets, produced by makers of component systems, combine into single units some of the components commonly sold separately. Compacts take up less room than component systems, and they come almost totally assembled. They range in price from about $350 to $600. The highest priced sets tend to perform as well as similarly priced component systems.

Component systems. These are the best. They come in components chosen and bought separately, then connected together by the buyer or, possibly for an extra fee, by a dealer. They permit the selection of units tailored to need or pocketbook. Basic to any system are amplifier and speaker components; beyond that a system may have a tape recorder and player, an AM-FM radio, a record player, or any combination of these. Assembly generally is not difficult. Even with one of the widely available discounts, it is hard to assemble a system for less than $350. Prices range to $1,800. Buyers should assess the quality of components before buying by checking books and periodicals that appraise hi-fi stereo equipment.

But the hi-fi stereo shopper needs a basic vocabulary of parts just to begin research. He should know that:

The *amplifier* increases the tiny flow of electricity generated by a tape player or record player to a level high enough to make the speakers function; a *preamplifier*, or preamp, sometimes is used to boost the sound signal headed for the amplifier. These components may come separately or assembled in a *receiver*, a device with numerous control knobs plus a *tuner*, a device that pulls in radio signals and converts them into intelligible sound. Tuners, essentially radios without amplifiers or speakers, also come separately.

The *cartridge* or *pickup,* one of the parts it is wise to let the dealer install, converts the mechanical movements of the *stylus,* or needle, into electrical impulses. With the stylus, it fits into the *tone arm,* which is fastened to a *turntable* base and holds the needle on the record. The turntable is the flat, circular plate that holds and rotates the record. When coupled with the tone arm and turntable, a *changer* feeds records onto the turntable automatically, making it possible to play stacks of records.

The *cabinet,* usually of wood or metal, houses the *chassis* of each major component and provides a decorative covering. The *tape deck* consists of a tape recorder and player that utilizes the stereo system's amplifier and speakers as the tuner does. A *kit* provides ingredients for do-it-yourselfers; they can save as much as 40 per cent of the total cost of a system by doing their own wiring and soldering.

Before buying a stereo set make a few tests. Turn the volume down as low as it will go. If a hum develops, forget that set. Borrow a test record featuring a full orchestra. Play it with the bass knob turned on full. The sound should be solid, not tinny. Turn off the bass and turn the treble knob up full. The sound should be clear —not dull or muffled.

Next, ask the dealer for a stroboscopic disc, a patterned disc used for testing turntables. If the pattern appears stationary, the turntable speed is accurate and constant. Also watch the tone arm to see if the turntable revolves evenly. Uneven rotation causes a sound called "flutter." Faulty turntables also produce a growling sound called "rumble." That and any excessive noise should disqualify a set.

Pianos: Key Notes for Buyers

THE addition of a piano to a household usually involves a substantial outlay of both money and home space. Pianos come in a broad variety of styles and sizes, and cost from $400 to $10,000.

Few family budgets will permit the purchase of a $10,000 piano, but it's possible to find a fine piano for much less. A beginner may avoid, or at least delay, a large expenditure by simply renting a piano from a music store until he's sure he wants to continue his pursuit. Often the monthly rental fee will be as low as 2 per cent of the price of the piano. If a customer decides to buy the piano, the rent will usually count toward purchase. Many companies, however, will limit the number of months a piano may be rented.

Within budget restrictions a good rule of thumb is to buy the largest piano available. The cost of a piano generally increases with its size, but so does the quality of its tone.

A prime factor in establishing tone is a piano's soundboard. It acts like a wooden membrane inside a piano to amplify sound. Keys trigger felt-covered hammers that hit wires or strings connected to the soundboard. A large soundboard does a better job of projecting piano music than a small one.

A grand piano, which has a soundboard running the length of its lid, should be measured horizontally from the keyboard to the end of its body or case. A vertical piano, with the soundboard standing at its back, should be measured from top to floor.

Prices of grand pianos begin at about $1,800 and their soundboards run to about nine feet. Experts agree that, in general, grands sound better than verticals, which have soundboards running to 3 feet 10 inches. But they warn that a grand piano less than five feet long may not be worth considering.

Verticals, which sell for $400 to $2,000, may be divided into three groups. At the top in price and size are professional or studio uprights. Consoles, one step below, rise to about 3½ feet. Spinets are about 3 feet tall.

Spinets have a peculiar disadvantage: They use a mechanism called a "drop action" to convert pressure on the keys to hammer blows on the strings. All other pianos, including grands, use a simpler device that is considered easier to maintain.

The manufacturer's name should be cast into the iron plate found under the strings. Models that lack this imprint are known in the trade as "stencil" pianos. Often they amount to little more than junk, and a retailer may stencil his own company name on them and represent them as quality instruments.

Avoid selecting a piano, too, that has a "laminated" soundboard. A fine piano—or even an average one— must have a soundboard made of solid spruce.

The best way to size up the quality of any piano is to play it. A novice may want to ask a friend who plays and has an ear for music to accompany him on his shopping trip. Any piano of reasonable quality ought to be able to produce both loud and soft sound, and each key should take the same amount of pressure to make an equal volume of sound. If some or all of the keys are very easy or very difficult to depress, a pianist may develop poor technique.

It's a good idea to check the piano pedals. Two are most often found: The left pedal mutes the tones and the right pedal sustains them.

Some models also offer a center pedal. It may be a true "sostenuto," which sustains the notes played just before it is pressed but doesn't hold those played afterwards. It may serve as a sostenuto only for the bass notes. Possibly, it will have the same effect as the right pedal, only more so. Or it may be a dummy.

The tonal quality of a piano, including the special effects produced by the pedals, probably will sound different after the instrument is moved out of the store into a living room, where sound may be dulled by carpets and curtains. To compensate, it may be wise to choose a piano that seems especially brilliant in a store.

Unlike violins, pianos don't improve in tone as they age. A piano has thousands of parts that gradually go out of order.

Depending on its condition and the whim of its owner, a second-hand piano may sell . . . for nearly its original price or next to nothing. Anyone in the market for a used piano should shop carefully.

The same criteria for judging new pianos should be used in selecting a used piano. A shopper must go one step further, however, and look for obvious signs of wear. If the hammers are flattened, rather than gently rounded, it may cost up to $200 to replace them so a piano won't sound tinny.

Not all of the assets or defects of a used piano are so obvious to an amateur. It's possible, for example, for a piano to have a soundboard with a crack that doesn't impair tone quality. It may be profitable to ask a piano tuner to appraise any used piano. He probably will charge $10 or $15 but it will be worth it if he steers you onto a bargain or away from a bad buy.

Once a piano is yours, it's important to keep it serviced. Experts disagree over how often a piano should be tuned, but many say that twice a year is the absolute minimum. During the first two years, while a new piano is being broken in, it may be necessary to have it tuned three or four times. Regular tuning is mandatory for a serious piano student; an out-of-tune piano may stunt the development of a musician's ear and discourage practicing.

Tuning probably will cost from $10 to $25 and, if a tuner is conscientious, should take at least an hour. A process known as "voicing" is available for about the same price from many tuners. It may make a piano sound brighter or more mellow and can bring out the sound of individual keys that have worn out or grown faint.

Less repair and tuning work is likely to be required if a piano is kept away from windows and heat or air-conditioning outlets.

LOOKING FOR SPOONS or other items to complete that heirloom set of silver flatware. No problem if it is sterling silver. The manufacturers retain molds and fill orders from time to time in any pattern they ever issued. However, silverplate replacements are hard to find once the manufacturers' inventories are gone. To meet the problem, a Denver couple maintains a stock of 50,000 pieces of discontinued silverplate. For information, write to Mr. and Mrs. Clay Crousen, The Silver Chest, P.O. Box 20072, Denver, Colo. 80220.

Mail Ordering –
Convenience and Problems

THE mail-order business holds a romantic position in U.S. history; its merchandise catalogs of yesteryear, originally distributed free, now sell in replica as prized Americana. Unlike the Pony Express and the paddlewheel steamers, this mail-order traffic has survived and thrived—so mightily that consumers now spend some $45 billion a year buying everything from metronomes to magazines by mail.

Yet customers—by the thousands—are complaining. Completely honest mail-order houses confess they are at times betrayed by their own computerized shops, and by Uncle Sam's mailmen. Well beyond that, evidence is accumulating that this lightly policed industry has become a harbor for "sloppy operators" and outright frauds, who mulct not only gullible poor folk but prosperous sophisticates.

Contemplate the plight of Darrell O. Poole, chief physicist at Mt. Sinai Hospital in Miami. Because he often works 12 to 14 hours a day, applying his electronics-engineering training and talents to the cause of healing, he finds catalog buying handy. But he tells this tale:

Mr. Poole mailed an order and his $355.75 check for hi-fi components to Electronic Values, Inc., New York City, on Dec. 6, 1969. He got his canceled check back—fast. The hi-fi paraphernalia still hasn't come.

He wrote repeatedly to the company and received no reply. He phoned; he reached the company once. But he was cut off after being told snappishly that his order was "en route." He has complained to the Federal Trade Commission, to the U.S. Postal Service, and to Mrs. Virginia Knauer, the President's special adviser on consumer affairs. No satisfaction.

In checking on the company, The National Observer found Electronic Values has moved from its store-front office at 85 W. Broadway, leaving no forwarding address. Says Mr. Poole: "I feel terrible."

Not everyone takes it so hard.

Bernard Novick, New York City attorney and numismatist, says he answered a New York Times advertisement for commemorative, U.S. bicentennial medallions, sending $75 to Wedgwood Mint of New Haven, Conn. He assertedly got back his canceled check; nothing more. Wedgwood Mint (not to be confused with the British makers of Wedgewood china) has been found guilty of mail fraud—but it is appealing the verdict.

A spokesman for the New York Times comments: "We make an earnest effort to keep only reliable advertisements in the paper. It disappoints us when a reader suffers from responding to our advertisements." Mr. Novick, who has been collecting coins by mail for 30 years, has swallowed his own disappointment. Says he: "This doesn't diminish my enthusiasm; I'll order by mail again."

For six years Bernard Gaer, owner of A-1 Kennels and Ozark Coonhound Kennels in Alma, Ark., has advertised mail-order hunting dogs in such national publications as Sports Afield, Field and Stream, and Outdoor Life.

R. A. Martindale of Warren, Ark., declares he paid $85 for two squirrel hunters he never got. Lowell D.

Cooper, Ashville, Ohio, reports he ordered a dog, sent a check for $60, and even wound up paying added shipping charges. The dog he received was assertedly blind in one eye and going blind in the other. Mr. Gaer and an associate have been indicted on 22 counts of mail fraud, and pleaded innocent.

Sports Afield and Field and Stream decline to comment on the incidents. Outdoor Life says it is not its policy to run the advertising of frauds. In fact, says August Small, advertising services manager: "Whenever we've forwarded consumer complaints to Mr. Gaer, he has immediately made good our readers' losses."

After spotting advertisements in Tucson's Arizona Star and in the Daily Citizen, which have been jointly managed newspapers, John S. Andrews, a Hughes Aircraft Co. executive in that city, ordered two suits from R. W. James Co. The company advertised itself as a mail-order dealer in Hong Kong-made men's attire.

Mr. Andrews assertedly paid $283.09 for his suits in 1968—and got a letter stating his shipment would be "delayed." But he says he still hasn't seen the suits. The U.S. district attorney's office in Phoenix reports that Robert James Ward, owner of the company, vanished from Arizona following his indictment and without entering a plea of innocence or guilt.

Says Mr. Andrews: "I do a lot of mail-order buying. I feel it was partly my own stupidity that hurt me here. I'll be more discriminating about the companies I deal with from now on." The advertising director of the Tucson papers explains his publications are discriminating themselves; and check on would-be advertisers. "Apparently these people (Ward and his company) checked out all right," he says.

As government officials and the mail-order industry are beginning to realize, a list like this could go on and on.

A 1970 report based on a five-city survey by the Federal Trade Commission (FTC) shows nondelivery of paid-for, mail-order merchandise ranks as consumers' number-one problem. Nearly 15 per cent of all complaints in the FTC survey dealt with nondelivery.

The FTC report took the industry and many consumer activists by surprise. John Daly, vice president of the Direct Mail Advertising Association, Inc., the industry's national trade organization, was incredulous when he heard the findings. Now he says: "Apparently the problem has existed a long time without our knowing it."

Evidence has been there.

In preparation for an interview, Betty Furness, the former Presidential aide and magazine columnist who directs New York's State Consumer Protection Board, had assistants survey her office's complaint files. She reports: "I have found that practically 20 per cent of our unsolicited mail deals directly with nondelivery. And I say, 'Wow!' "

Newspaper "action-line" columnists like Don Carter of the Seattle Post-Intelligencer, Roy Courtade of the Detroit News, and Tim Mehren of California's Sacramento Bee receive voluminous mail concerning the problem in their areas. Mr. Carter says he received 2,000 mail-order complaints in 1970.

Protests have been arriving at the offices of Mrs. Knauer, the President's consumer adviser. Her "1970 Mail-Order" folder of onionskin copies of responses sent to consumers is three inches thick. Many of the complainants sent Mrs. Knauer duplicates of canceled checks, insisting that they never received their merchandise.

Mrs. Knauer's office does not investigate these allegations, nor does it have authority to prosecute offenders. It forwards some jeremiads that complain of outright cheating to the Postal Service or Trade Commission, and it may or may not learn what subsequently happens. More routine laments go directly to the companies involved—with notes requesting action. Generally companies report back, stating that matters have been "adjusted."

Respectable companies — small and large—in the business of selling and delivering by mail do strive to rectify justified complaints, of course. Edward Shade, head of the mail-order division of renowned Abercrombie and Fitch, notes that his firm "and other reputable ones" also try to forestall them.

They quickly send cards to assure buyers an order has been received. They keep sizable inventories. When a rush of orders exhausts stocks, so goods can't be sent to arrive in a week or so, a letter goes out explaining why. Often the companies phone customers. "We might not call about a $12.50 item; we probably would phone about a $25 order if the customer weren't more than, say, 400 miles away. A couple of weeks ago we called a buyer in Seward, Alaska.

"Still," muses the executive, "I must agree there are problems in this business that will always be with us, and they do cause consternation."

Giants of the trade such as Sears, Roebuck and Montgomery Ward reluctantly admit they hear some howls from customers. Sears alone generates around $2 billion annually in mail-order sales. "With that magnitude of orders," observes an official, "we would have a number of irregularities." But both Sears and Montgomery Ward, like many other mail retailers, refuse to give statistics on complaints.

More open is Columbia House, formerly CBS Direct Marketing Services of the CBS broadcasting system, where an official reports receipt of about 1,500,000 legitimate complaints a year. Columbia House operates two record clubs; it has about 2,000,000 customers and an estimated 50,000,000 customer transactions yearly.

The National Observer finds itself in the thick of the mail-order business, in two ways. First, a sizable proportion of this newspaper's advertising space is taken up by mail-order firms; The Observer's customer-relations department in New York says it gets around 20 protests a week from readers who have responded to various advertisements and say their orders have not yet been filled satisfactorily.

Second, and more directly, more than 500,000 copies of The Observer are printed each week and most of these are delivered by mail; new mail orders flow in constantly. According to figures of The Observer's circulation-service department, some 3,500 "complaint and inquiry letters" were received in just one recent month, January. No calculations are available on how many customers complained of nondelivery, but many did.

A more recent count, for March, showed 956 customer communications about non-receipt of this newspaper. A company spokesman said some were concerned with delivery lapses caused by late renewals, changes of address and post office snafus. Others came from new subscribers impatient with delays in starting delivery. In the first five business days of April, a special count showed 59 letters were received from new subscribers complaining they'd sent in their money but had not yet got the paper. Exactly the same number, as it happened, wrote in to say they were by error getting two copies each week instead of one.

Business spokesmen for The Observer offer much

the same explanations of their own delivery problems as do many other mail-order suppliers: human error, cantankerous computers (and other office equipment), and the U.S. Postal Service.

When many of its packages strayed, Ambassador Leather Goods, Tempe, Ariz., undertook an investigation in conjunction with postal inspectors. It found that postmen were relabeling packages and sending them to friends, relatives, and to other places where they could be opened and their contents stolen.

Theft by mailmen "is a growing problem," notes an internal Postal Service publication called the Postal Leader. So is theft by others from mail-order firm delivery rooms, from house porches and mail boxes. But postmen get the blame for that, too, the Leader laments.

Still, there are other reasons for nondelivery. Many mail-order merchants habitually lay in only small stocks of newly advertised items, run out, and fail to reorder in sufficient volume to keep up with some "hot" lines of their business—or find factories unable or unwilling to produce what's needed.

Many other operators — again including honest ones—carry no stocks at all. These are the "drop shippers," who accept orders from customers and send them on to manufacturers for shipment. They may not know how much of a product a manufacturer has on hand, or even whether the factory will continue making it. A drop shipper can be getting orders months after a product is off the market.

No one knows whether these and other foibles of reputable companies are causing most consumer vexations, or whether gypsters are multiplying. Mr. Daly of the industry association blames the gypsters.

"Anyone can get into this business," he grumbles.

"Without intending to fulfill orders, they get checks and grab big money in a short time. And fraud is hard to prove."

That's true. Industry sources say mail-order houses often get orders from 2 to 3 per cent or more of those they send catalogs to. That's why catalogs are desirable sales vehicles, and that's why it wouldn't take long for the nondeliverer to pocket a profit before vanishing.

Anyone, including the gyp, can buy a "preprinted catalog" from one of 24 companies. He inserts a self-addressed order form, obtains a mailing list for a few cents a name, and sets up as a "mail-order house."

Or by judiciously editing and clipping existing catalogs, the devious entrepreneur can compile a catalog of his own. It might be a "special" book, listing only hi-fi or camping gear, for example.

The chief deterrent against mail-order crooks is the Postal Service's Fraud Branch. But it has only 120 investigators scattered throughout the 50 states. They must investigate all postal fraud cases, not just mail-order matters. At recent count the branch had 643 investigations under way—5 1-3 per man.

William J. Cotter, chief postal inspector, says the law requires proof of intent to defraud. Thus the merchant who fills most orders but pockets a few can get away with it as long as he doesn't establish a "pattern of deceit."

Moreover, Mr. Cotter says, the law's deterrent is weak: a $1,000 fine or five years in jail, or both. That deterrent isn't used much either. "There are a lot of light fines, suspended sentences, and probations given," Mr. Cotter notes.

Indeed there are.

Paul Allen Seguin of Richmond, Mich., was convicted of failure to deliver the "mint-condition" Model A

Ford parts he offered for sale in various automotive magazines. His sentence: two years probation and a $200 fine.

Harry Supera and Ronald L. Singer, operating in Baltimore as Eastern Consumer Co. and as Baltimore Wholesale Distributors, pleaded guilty to mail frauds involving concealment of finance charges in letters and "flyers" sent to consumers. Their sentences: probation for three years.

Gerald Leslie Bradley, owner of Surplus Jobbers, Inc., Humboldt, Iowa, admitted selling by mail used Jeeps "in good running condition." He also admitted he owned no Jeeps to sell. Sentence: probation for five years.

Richard H. Boyce was one of 11 men involved in a 50-count mail-fraud indictment involving Marketing Specialists of America, Inc., of Baltimore. The men were accused of failing to deliver desk-size, battery-operated telephone indexes—fancy gadgets priced as high as $96 each. Would-be buyers allegedly lost $1,000,000 in the scheme. Boyce, first to stand trial, did not contest the charge. His sentence: probation for two years.

Though the postal force apparently has no big plans for intensifying its crackdowns, consumer furor may find a response elsewhere in government. Staff men at the Federal Trade Commission have been studying the feasibility of regulating the industry, and one official reports that commissioners may soon get a report recommending action. An agency attorney suggests the report may propose rules similar to those outlined in February by New York City's consumer-protection agency for implementation in that metropolis.

The New York City agency proposes making it illegal for a company to accept mail orders or payment for merchandise unless it ships or delivers the goods within six weeks. Failure to do so would require the merchant to make an automatic refund or to notify the buyer and offer him his money back. Mail-order transactions involving open-end credit purchases and the sale of certain periodicals would be exempted.

A hint that mail-order houses might be regulated locally came when New York Attorney General Louis Lefkowitz won an injunction against Bevis Industries, Inc., which he said was doing business under such names as J. P. Darby, Esq.; Readers' World Press Club; Dione Lucas; Hobi, Inc.; Maison Michel, Ltd.; Executive House; and others.

The unprecedented decision skirted the fraud issue. It was based on general business laws. That became possible when Bevis admitted such acts as failure to deliver merchandise in a reasonable time; misstatement of prices; and advertising items were "on sale" when they were not.

At one point, Mr. Lefkowitz alleged, the company fell behind in filling orders for 1,300 out-of-stock items. Yet it continued to offer them for sale while advertising prompt delivery.

Several of the companies named in the Bevis case have advertised in The National Observer, which afterward rejected their advertising for a time. Following the corporation's public pledge to reform and changes in its executive staffing, its companies' advertisements are being accepted once more.

The Bevis enterprises have been viewed with less than wholehearted enthusiasm, however, by the Direct Mail Advertising Association. Within recent weeks Hobi, Inc., a Bevis holding, applied for membership in the trade group and was refused, according to Robert F. DeLay, association president.

This trade organization considers its "moral persuasion" a deterrent to industry malpractice. It represents only some 1,600 of the 4,000 to 5,000 companies it estimates to be in the business. Its officials try to screen out undesirables by checking the reputations of the 170 to 200 firms seeking membership each year. "We wind up rejecting two, maybe three," says vice president John Daly.

Recently, association officials have mailed to members special letters, calling attention to critical press and consumer-group statements about the industry and reminding the membership of the association's ethical code. It has prepared a list of association members for consumers who wish to deal exclusively with DMAA-sanctioned companies.

Each year the organization confronts five, perhaps six, members for purported violations of its code of ethics, and it secures from them promises to reform. Those refusing to shape up can be expelled.

Yet since the association's founding—in 1917—only one member has been dismissed—and not for non-delivery of what he promised. That was Ralph Ginzburg, founder of Eros magazine, the newsletter Liaison, and other erotic publications.

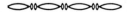

BULK MEAT PURCHASING doesn't always save money. An unscrupulous dealer can load an unwary buyer down with a large section of meat containing so much fat, bone, or low-grade meat that the per-pound cost of edible portions may exceed the cost of an individual cut at a retail market. Significant savings are possible, however, on bulk cuts sold by reputable dealers or purchased by knowledgeable buyers. Helpful advice on bulk purchasing is contained in "How to Buy Meat for Your Freezer," Home and Garden Bulletin No. 166, a Department of Agriculture booklet available for 20 cents from the Government Printing Office, Washington, D.C. 20402.

Finding a Corking Good Wine

AMERICANS drink more than a gallon of wine per person each year. Fewer and fewer persons are limiting wine drinking to a few very special occasions. Even so, the country has a way to go to close the wine-consuming gap between such Old World countries as France, where per capita consumption is 30 times the U.S. figure.

And an American in a wine shop tends to be timid and uncertain. He faces the problem of choosing from among scores of brands and types of wines; probably he has read somewhere that the true wine lover must be very knowledgeable about the area in which the grapes for a particular wine were grown, their vintage or the year in which they were harvested, and the proper type of wine to accompany a particular food. He may worry that a good wine is by definition a high-priced wine or that he will need a special storage area at home to properly keep his wine.

There are wine lovers who make a lifetime hobby of the subject and who make an elaborate ritual of buying, storing, and drinking wine. But there are millions of wine lovers, including Europeans, who dispense with the ritual and find and enjoy moderate- and low-cost wines.

A novice may want to read a book or pamphlet about wine. Most libraries and book stores have a wealth of materials on the subject. Among the more useful books are: *Encyclopedia of Wine*, by Frank

Schoonmaker, Hastings House Publishers, Inc., 151 E. 50th St., New York City 10022, $6.95; and *Guide to Wines, Spirits, and Beers,* by Harold J. Grossman, Charles Scribner's Sons, 597 5th Ave., New York City 10017, $8.95.

In reading any book about wines, be alert for outdated references to specific bottles and prices. The price of a bottle of wine made from a particular year's grapes can go up or down as a wine grows older, depending on how well the wine "matures." Retail prices also vary from one area to another, often because of different tax rates.

Some books emphasize or discuss only imported wines. Free literature from the Wine Institute, 717 Market St., San Francisco, Calif. 94103 is pretty well confined to wines produced in California. So, if you wish to learn a bit about a variety of wines, make sure your literature includes information on California and New York State wines as well as the products from Europe.

After a beginner learns that Burgundy, *Pinot Noir,* claret, and Medoc describe red table wines, while Chablis, *Pouilly Fuisse,* sauterne, and *Pinot Chardonnay* refer to white table wines, he is ready to buy and compare to find the one he likes.

You may want to begin by trying only California wines, sampling various reds, whites, and roses (row-ZAYS) or pink wines to learn their sometimes explicit but often subtle differences. Then you might compare California wines with those from New York and from across the Atlantic to see how wines can taste different even if they have similar or identical names.

You should find, for instance, that a California Burgundy is not like New York Burgundy, and that neither one is much like a wine from the Burgundy region of France. Also compare different vintages of the same wines if they are listed on the bottle; see if there is a significant difference to you. Bottles not showing vintage years probably are blends of wines from different harvests.

A good way to sample a lot of wines at minimum expense is to hold a wine-tasting party. Invite friends who also want to learn more about wines—you may be surprised at how many are interested—and have them bring along a bottle or two. You might simplify things by limiting testing to all reds or all whites. Get a supply of small glasses, prepare plates of cheese and crackers, and you're all set. You may want to take notes about the wines.

Domestic table wine is sold most often in bottles containing 25.6 fluid ounces (one-fifth of a gallon) with a price range from a little over $1 to $2. Imported wines, usually in 24-ounce sizes, cost from $2 or $3 up to $25 or more for the most highly prized bottles. But don't be afraid to try wines from Spain, Portugal, France, or elsewhere that cost under $2; you may find one you like better than some costing much more.

And look for domestic wines you like in larger bottles. A fifth of Almaden Mountain Red Burgundy sells in some areas for about $1.30. You can get more than twice as much wine in a half-gallon (64-ounce) jug for about $2 and a full gallon (128 ounces) for about $3.50.

Don't expect wine to always keep the same taste after it has been opened a short time or stored a long time. Experts emphasize that wine is a living thing; it reacts to microorganisms in air, and also can spoil if exposed to too much heat, light, or agitation. But a few precautions should head off spoilage. Keep the wine in a relatively cool, quiet corner. Laying a bottle on its side will keep the cork moist and air-tight. Some bottles have screw tops and can be kept upright.

If all the contents of a half-gallon or gallon jug are not to be used within a few days after opening it, you can pour the wine gently into clean, smaller bottles to be corked and stored for later use. Refrigeration will help keep a recorked, partly used bottle of wine fresh.

Don't be too concerned about how to drink wines with meals. Most wine drinkers prefer red wines at room temperature with red meats and hearty meals, and chilled white wines with lighter, more delicately flavored meats, fish, and other foods. Chilled rose is served commonly with about any meal. Remember, you are your own expert on what you like.

AN AUTOMATIC LAWNMOWER, which unattended can mow up to 7,500 square feet of lawn, has been put on the market by Mowbot, Inc., 9 Hackett Dr., Tonawanda, N.Y. 14150. The mower is driven by a self-contained, 12-volt, rechargeable battery. The area to be mowed is outlined by a wire, which gives off an electronic signal. As the mower approaches the wire, sensors pick up the signal and send the mower off on a new course. The random courses eventually mow all of the lawn section within the wire. The mower will stop if it encounters an object. Cutting blades are on the perimeter of two whirling discs beneath the mower. The blades pivot when they strike a rock or other hard object, minimizing the danger of sending such objects whizzing across the lawn. The cost of lazing while the Mowbot cuts the lawn: about $795.

TANK-TYPE insecticide sprayers should be thoroughly rinsed with clean water after each use to minimize corrosion. A tank weakened by corrosion may burst explosively when a user pressurizes it by operating the built-in air pump. After a tank has been cleaned, pressurize it slightly and allow clean water to flush the spray hose and nozzle. When storing a sprayer, release all pressure, remove the air pump, and hang the tank upside down for drainage.

The Ins and Outs of Bourbon

Bourbon is the best-selling whisky in the United States, a two-to-one favorite over Scotch. It also is the only liquor ever designated by the United States Congress as "a distinctive product of the United States," and the only American-made spirit given the same international protection that is accorded Scotch and cognac by the *Federation Internationale de Vins et Spiriteaux*, the 14-nation organization of wine and spirit distillers that lays down the law on what may be called what in the world liquor market.

Bourbon is only bourbon when it is made in the United States. In England, where bourbon is the new "in" drink, it is often sipped after dinner as though it were a fine cognac.

Many Americans know little if anything about bourbons and how to choose the one that best suits their taste buds and pocketbooks. With over 200 brands on the market, not including the thousands of private brands that liquor stores now stock, this is no easy matter. True bourbon fanciers will tell you they can tell one bourbon from another, but the average customer likely will sympathize with the young liquor-store clerk who recently concluded: "Sure, I can tell the difference. I can tell the difference the morning after. If it wasn't a good bourbon, I'll know it."

Bourbon gets its name from the county, now in Kentucky, where the Rev. Elijah Craig, a flax-mill owner and part-time Baptist minister, first concocted the stuff back in 1789. To make a good bourbon, you need plenty of good corn grain and iron-free water that has filtered through limestone. For this reason, most of the industry's distilleries are built along a single limestone belt that runs from Kentucky to the Illinois-Indiana corn belt. Bourbon also is distilled in California, Georgia, Virginia, and Pennsylvania.

All bourbons have a caramel-sweet flavor and reddish-brown color, but there are subtle differences. Bourbon is, by U.S. law, a straight whisky made from a fermented mash of not less than 51 per cent nor more than 79 per cent corn grain. With 80 per cent corn in the mash, you have corn whisky; with less than 51 per cent you have something else, a blended whisky, perhaps, or a rye whisky, since rye is the "small-grain" ingredient in all bourbon mashes.

Bourbon brewers long ago found that the more corn grain in the mash, the lighter will be the body of the whisky. Formula information is never given on a label. Distillers' secrets include such factors as properties of the yeast used in the fermenting process, the proof at which the whisky was distilled (the higher the lighter), or the conditions under which the bourbon was aged.

All bourbons, again by U.S. law, are distilled at no higher than 160 proof and are reduced to 125 proof or less before being aged. Proof is a measure of alcoholic content and equals twice the percentage of alcohol in whisky; a 100-proof whisky would be 50 per cent alcohol. Bourbon aging, by law, must be for not less than two years in charred, new oak barrels. It is almost impossible, however, to buy a bourbon that has been aged less than four years. And age is not always a key to quality. A bourbon left too long in a barrel will take on a woody flavor. It also is possible to design bourbon mashes to come to maturity at predetermined times. The percentage of rye in the mash affects the rate at which a whisky matures, for example. So does the thickness or thinness of the char on the barrel. Bourbons aged in barrels with thick char reach their peak in flavor, bouquet, and color faster than bourbons aged in thinly charred barrels.

Ostensibly there is a difference between "sourmash" and "sweet-mash" bourbons. But sour-mash is simply bourbon that includes in its ingredients a little leftover mash—fermented but not distilled—from the distiller's preceding batch. This is called "spent distiller's brew," and it slows down the fermentation process and makes it easier for the distiller to maintain a continuity of taste in his whisky. According to an official of the Bourbon Institute, the distillers' trade association, only one distiller is "suspected" of not using sour mash in his bourbon. Many distillers don't advertise their use of sour mash.

A few distillers advertise some of their products as "charcoal filtered," which means that during the distilling process the whisky has been filtered through charcoal to remove what some distillers feel are undesirable elements in the brew. Other distillers will tell you the process also removes valuable flavor elements. "Probably 99 per cent of the bourbon on today's market has been charcoal filtered in one way or another, though the labels may not say so," says another Bourbon Institute official.

The U.S. Government affidavit, "Bottled in Bond," on a bottle of bourbon is no guarantee of quality. It merely confirms that the whisky inside is at least four years old and was bottled at 100 proof. The Government can attest to this because —largely for tax purposes but also to see that each detail of the bourbon law is obeyed

—it is in on every step of the bourbon-making process. Visitors to bourbon distilleries are always surprised to find as many Government men as distillery employes milling about the place. Sometimes more. Government men check the mash that goes into a still and the bourbon that comes out; they keep the keys to the warehouses where the aging whisky is stored. And when aged whisky is "dumped" from its barrels at the end of the long aging process, they're there to measure it again, since bourbon increases about one proof unit a year in the barrel.

Americans tend more and more to favor light whiskies. The 100-proof bottled-in-bond bourbons account for less than 10 per cent of today's bourbon sales. The real bourbon lover who buys 86-proof bourbon for its lightness, however, may be missing a bargain. Bourbon, says a Bourbon Institute expert, should always be diluted half-and-half with water; 100-proof straight whisky will paralyze your taste buds. And as long as you're diluting the alcohol, you get more of it to dilute in a 100-proof bottle, with its 50 per cent alcohol, than you get in an 86-proof bottle with its ratio of 43 per cent alcohol to 57 per cent distilled water.

Bourbon is primarily a sippin' whisky, as any bourbon lover will tell you, but he'll also tell you that bourbon makes the best mixed drinks because it has so much *character*. It's a good cooking whisky, too, says the Bourbon Institute. It has a special affinity for beef and chocolate. If you add bourbon to your meals, however, be sure to count the one calorie per proof per ounce that any distilled spirit adds to your diet. Recipes for bourbon mixed drinks and cookery are available in some liquor stores or from the Bourbon Institute, 277 Park Ave., New York, N.Y. 10017.

Beer Put to the Taste Test

Americans drink nearly 4,000,000,000 gallons of domestic beer a year, about 29½ gallons for every adult. In addition, they downed roughly 25,-000,000 gallons of imported beer.

Anheuser-Busch, Inc., is their favorite brewer. Yet a taste test indicates that it is unlikely that a Budweiser fan can pick the brand from among other major U.S. brands when all are served in plain glasses.

When it comes to choosing between the major beers, price is as good a guide as anything. Even some beer-industry officials say that differences in taste between beers usually can be detected only by connoisseurs with taste perceptions typical beer drinkers can't match. National Observer tests bear this out.

A small group of brand-conscious beer drinkers participated in the tests. The goal was to discover if the members of the group really could, as they contended, distinguish between various beers. They were tested on whether they could differentiate between domestic brands, between bottled regular beer and canned beer of the same brand, between foreign brands, and between foreign and domestic beers.

The tests involved first tasting without swallowing and then both tasting and swallowing. Omitted from the tests were heavy, less effervescent brews like Lowenbrau Dark because they are not national favorites and none was drunk regularly by any of the participants. However, both "light-bodied" brands like Budweiser and "medium-bodied" brands like Miller High Life were intermingled in the tests.

When given Carling Black Label, Miller High Life, and Budweiser in different, unmarked glasses, half the tasters said the glasses contained the same brand of beer. The other half said two glasses contained the same beer and one held a different brew. They disagreed on which glass contained the "different" one. Nor could they consistently tell the difference between bottled draft and regular bottled beer.

Half the group noted a distinction between canned and bottled beer. All recognized a difference between domestic and foreign beers and between several foreign brands.

The testers generally liked the beers they sampled. They said the difference between the domestic and foreign brands generally wasn't great. That coincides with the statement of a Brewers Association of America spokesman, who says the main discernible difference between domestic and imported beer is price.

Price varies from region to region and city to city, and prices can fluctuate from week to week. Beer costs more almost everywhere in July and August.

Generally it costs more when bought from a small store than it does when purchased at supermarkets, which sell nearly half of the beer sold. Food stores in some areas hawk beer at special low prices, using the product as a crowd puller.

Most beer Americans consume is *lager,* a German word meaning "storage." And it's the method of storage or aging that marks lager from ale.

All beer is made from malted cereal, often barley malt, mixed with water and with yeast, the fermenting catalyst. In concocting lager, the brewer uses yeast that settles to the bottom of the fermenting tank after fermentation. At this point the fluid is a cloudy, immature, "green" beer. The green beer is piped into tanks where it is stored at near-freezing temperatures for several months to clear up and mellow.

Ale, a stronger drink, is made with yeast that stays on the top of the fermenting fluid. It is fermented and aged differently.

Pilsener beer is a kind of lager that supposedly resembles in taste and appearance a beer commonly brewed in Pilsen, Czechoslovakia. It and Dortmund-type lager are generally characterized by pale color, medium bitterness, and rather high carbonation.

Vienna and Munich-type beers have a darker hue, fuller body, and a sweeter taste than Pilseners. Bock, still another lager, is brewed in winter for spring consumption. It resembles Munich beer somewhat, but it is darker and heavier than the Munich and has a sweeter malt taste.

The alcoholic content of lagers varies little. It hovers around 4 per cent by weight, contrasted with 43 per cent alcohol by weight in 86-proof whiskies. Beers normally aren't rated by "proof." If they were, they would range from 8 to 10 proof with the foreign beers having the higher alcoholic content.

Alcoholic content isn't as important to many drinkers as the gas content of beer. That's because the carbon-dioxide gas, which gives beer its effervescence, can make the drinker feel stuffed.

Brewers insist drinkers themselves may be at fault for excess gas in their beer. They may have poured it too gently. Beer shouldn't be eased down the side of a tilted glass; it should be splashed into the center of the glass to help dispel the carbon dioxide. That way the drinker feels less full; he can drink more and burp less, say the brewers.

Selecting a Home Typewriter

THE person who wants to buy a typewriter for home use will find that he can spend as little as $30 or up to $240 or more for a new machine, and something less for a used one.

The typical typewriter is kept for about 20 years. So the prospective buyer would do well to be aware of the important factors that dictate price and quality differences, since he is likely to live with his typewriter for some time.

The price differences in typewriters are based on three main factors: the type of machine, whether lightweight portable or sophisticated electric; the extra convenience features it possesses; and where it is purchased, whether discount outlet or typewriter dealer.

There are four basic types of home-use typewriters, each with its own price range and advantages:

The very small, "featherweight" portables are priced from $29 to $75 and weigh from 8 to 10 pounds. Their drawbacks usually include a minimum of operating conveniences, a tendency to produce uneven lines of type, to "creep" on the table during use, and to require more energy and work in their use. They might be preferred by a constant traveler, the occasional typewriter user, or someone with a budget problem.

The full-size manual portable is priced from $70 to $130 and weighs 15 to 18 pounds. Its main advantages over the electric portable are less frequent and less expensive service. The manual portable may also withstand the stress of frequent travel better, and it can be used without regard to availability of electrical outlets.

The electric portable is priced from about $99 to $240, and weighs 20 to 30 pounds. Main advantages: Each key hits the paper with uniform pressure, resulting in more evenly printed copy; it can make up to 10 readable carbons, compared with about 5 on a manual; and it requires about 3 ounces of pressure to move a key, versus up to 3½ pounds on a manual.

The used, standard-size typewriter ranges in price from about $30 to $200. These machines usually are restored to nearly their original working condition. They are far more durable than most portables and might be preferred in a home with several children learning to type or where the machine will receive very heavy use.

Within each category, price progresses from lowest to highest mainly on the basis of the extra features the machines offer. The higher-priced machines will usually offer a combination of conveniences such as the half-space for insertion of forgotten letters, extra keys, or the option for interchangeable type, offering technical symbols.

The price goes up considerably on two particularly expensive features. One is longer carriage length. Standard size is 9½ or 10 inches. A longer length of 12 to 13 inches raises the price about $20 on both manuals and electrics, but allows paper to be inserted on its long side for typing graphs and charts.

The other expensive feature is a power return carriage in an electric portable. It raises the price $40 to $50, but means the fingers can be kept in typing position at all times, rather than using a lever to return the carriage to the start of a line.

The tabulator, which provides automatic paragraph spacing and lines up tabular material in charts, often is missing in the lightweight, least expensive portables. This can be an important convenience.

Another major price factor is where a machine is purchased. For example, the Smith-Corona electric with manual return and a 10-inch carriage, usually costs about $170 at a typewriter shop. A very similar version cost about $50 less in discount stores. Smith-Corona Marchant also makes many of Sears and all of Penney's typewriters. The Sears version of the $170 machine costs about $125.

There are several reasons not to count the typewriter dealer out despite his higher prices. Often he stocks several high-quality brands that are rarely available from discount sources. Although more expensive, these machines often offer superior smoothness and durability. Such brands include Adler, Facit, Hermes, Olivetti and Olympia.

The typewriter dealer also can discuss technical points, which the discount-store clerk usually cannot do.

The dealer unboxes and services the machine before delivery, a procedure that is often necessary before the machine will operate at its best. At discount outlets, the purchaser usually gets the typewriter still in its shipping carton. However, the buyer should ask that the typewriter be unboxed and tested before he takes it home, since even unpacking it can be a difficult undertaking for the novice.

Another important advantage the dealer offers is personal service on repairs. A dealer who also has a factory-authorized repair facility often tends to give priority to typewriters he has sold over those purchased at discount outlets.

In evaluating the various machines, here are some

points suggested by an official of the National Office Machine Dealers Association:

✔ The "feel" of the machine. This is the most important quality check. Type on several brands consecutively. There will probably be noticeable differences in the smoothness and "solidness" of their operations. The "tinny" echoing or the rattle that occurs in some brands means poor engineering that can cause annoyance during usage.

✔ Basket shift. When the key for capitalizing letters is pressed, it will either raise the platen (the roller that holds the paper) or it will depress the "basket" containing the keys. Lowering the basket is preferable and signifies a higher quality machine. It will mean quicker, more even operation.

✔ Two-color ribbon capability. Elimination of the option for changing ribbon colors probably means that the maximum number of corners has been cut in the machine's construction.

✔ Carriage return. A smooth, noiseless return suggests high-quality engineering. A ratchety sound may be a sign of less-than-best quality.

✔ Diameter of the platen. A very small roller will mean eventual problems with slipping paper, plus inconvenience in loading with stiff paper or envelopes.

✔ Carrying case. A cheap zipper or flimsy material often reflects low over-all quality.

Good care is important for any home typewriter. Keep it clean. Cover it when it is not in use. Don't let eraser bits fall into it. Wipe the platen periodically with denatured alcohol. Clean the type face with type cleaner. And have the machine oiled periodically by a repairman.

Mobile Homes for
Quick, Cheap Housing

THE construction of conventional homes costing $20,000 or less has dwindled almost to the vanishing point. Many couples with modest means, particularly young persons, are being forced into apartment living when they would prefer home ownership. Some, though, are turning to mobile homes in their search for moderately priced dwellings they can call their own.

Prices of mobile homes vary from about $4,000 to more than $15,000. The Mobile Homes Manufacturers Association lists the following price ranges, which include extra appliances or credit costs, for three major types of homes:

✔. $4,000 to $8,000 for a single unit. The unit may be 8 to 14 feet wide and 29 to 75 feet long. The most common size is 12 by 60 feet. (The length of a mobile home includes the length of a three-foot towing hitch on the front and the width will include any overhang.) The 12-by-60 unit usually has two bedrooms, one or two bathrooms, a kitchen, a dining area, and a living room.

✔ $4,500 to $9,000 for an expansible unit. This is a single unit with one or two sections, about 6 by 10 feet, that fold out from the side of the unit to make it L-shaped or, if there are two fold-out sections, to make it F- or U-shaped. A fold-out section is designed to increase the size of a bedroom or living room.

✔ $8,000 to $15,000 for a double-wide unit. A double-wide unit is made from two single units. The single units have special floor plans so that half of the double-wide unit doesn't duplicate the other. Most double-wide units have two or three bedrooms, some double-wide units, called sections, don't come on wheels and have to be transported by other vehicles.

It may be easier to get a loan for a mobile home than for a conventional home. But terms of mobile-home loans are usually less favorable to the borrower. The maximum period is about 12 years. Interest rates are the equivalent of about 12 to 14 per cent. Most lenders require a down payment of 20 to 30 per cent of the mobile-home cost.

The Federal Housing Administration (FHA) has been authorized to insure mobile-home loans. The insurance will cover loans of up to $10,000 for up to 12 years for single-width homes or loans up to $15,000 for up to 15 years for double-width homes. Interest is from 7.97 to 10.57 per cent, depending on the amount of a loan. Minimum down-payment is 5 per cent on a home costing up to $6,000 and 10 per cent for more expensive homes.

The Veterans Administration (VA) has a loan-guarantee program for mobile homes placed permanently on land owned by a veteran. The VA will guarantee a loan up to 30 per cent of the VA-appraised value of home and real estate, with a maximum of $17,500. The maximum term for a VA loan is 15 years and interest must not exceed 10.75 per cent for the home or 7 per cent for the land.

Mobile homes may be kept on private property, subject to local zoning restrictions, or in mobile-home parks. Parks charge about $40 to $60 a month in rent, excluding utilities. The average rent in the more than

20,000 parks in the country is $40, according to the Mobile Home Manufacturers Association. A directory of the some 12,000 mobile home parks is available for $3.95 from Woodall Publishing Co., 500 Hyacinth Place, Highland Park, Ill. 60035.

The basic services usually provided at average rates include: trash collection, sewage disposal, street lights, paved roads, a front-door walkway, automobile parking space, and water, electricity, and gas outlets.

Retail mobile-home dealers will often arrange to have a home transported from factory to homesite. The transportation charge is determined by the size of the home, the distance traveled, and the route. Tolls and special permits required in certain states will be added. The average cost is about $1 a mile. Some states require a "flag car" to drive ahead of an unusually wide home to warn oncoming motorists of the width hazard. A flag car can add 30 cents a mile to transportation costs.

Most mobile homes are furnished at the factories. A specially requested unfurnished home should cost appreciably less than the furnished model.

The furniture that comes with a mobile home usually will not be enough to fill the rooms and may be flimsy. Typically it includes: a table and four chairs for the dining area; springs and a mattress and sometimes a dresser for each bedroom; and a davenport, easy chair, coffee table, end table, and lamp for the living room. Curtains and wall-to-wall carpeting may be included.

Factory-installed appliances usually include an oven, range, refrigerator, water heater, and furnace. Others such as a dishwasher, clothes washer, and dryer are optional.

Joint Funds Not Always
Quickly Available

IF you share a joint bank account with your wife or husband, you may be assuming that when one of you dies, the other will have immediate ownership of and continued access to the funds. Many survivors have found out too late that the assumption often is incorrect. They have been barred from accounts just when they most need the money in them to meet funeral bills and other emergency expenses. When it is the husband who has died the problem often is acute because a family's primary income may have been stopped.

The problem stems from state tax laws. Funds passing from the deceased to the spouse usually are subject to state transfer or inheritance taxes, despite their inclusion in joint checking or savings accounts. Tax authorities may regard funds in a joint account as actually belonging to one spouse, usually the husband, with the other spouse merely having permission from the owner to make withdrawals.

Thus, a joint account does not necessarily mean joint ownership of its contents. The ownership may depend instead on which person deposits the money, or at least the majority of the money.

When a bank learns of the death of either of the holders of a joint account, it is required in most states to stop further withdrawals temporarily. This gives state authorities time to inspect the account and determine what taxes are to be assessed. It may take several weeks to obtain such a tax clearance, creating an inconvenience for some surviving spouses and perhaps a financial crisis for others.

Many states, however, have provisions in their laws to permit small emergency withdrawals up to several hundred dollars, subject to later taxation. Or there may be other provisions to eliminate or soften the effects of temporarily locking up joint-account funds.

Ask your bank what the law is in your state and how it would apply in your situation. Find out how much money one spouse could expect to withdraw in the few days immediately following the death of the other.

Then try to determine what expenses would be faced in the period between the time of death and the time full access to the funds would be gained. Some couples pay for burial plots, caskets, and other funeral expenses ahead of time. If you have not, and don't want to, be sure the necessary funds will be available when they are needed. And remember that bills for housing, utilities, food, and clothing go on.

What about life insurance? Will your company pay immediately upon receipt of proof of death? Consider other payments that will be made after you or your spouse dies, as from Social Security or employment benefits.

If your widow is likely to be short of cash immediately after your death, consider setting up an emergency checking or savings account in her name only. Barring some unusual circumstance, the money in it will be continually and readily available to her.

You may want to consult a lawyer who is familiar with local tax laws. He should also be able to help you determine what delays you will face and what your immediate expenses will be after your spouse's death. Whatever you may do, a little planning now can save a great deal of unnecessary aggravation after your or your spouse's death.

DANGEROUS ELECTRICAL SHOCKS may result when indoor appliances—such as vacuum cleaners—are used outside. Because they are normally used inside the home, such appliances seldom are grounded. Yet you could get a severe shock if they happen to leak electricity at the point where you touch them and if you are directly or indirectly touching damp earth, concrete, outdoor carpeting, a water or gas pipe, or even an electrical conductor touching one of them. Avoid the danger by grounding all indoor appliances you may be using outside. Use a three-wire power cord and three-prong plug. It also may be necessary to install three-prong receptacles. But you probably will have to call an electrician for that.

AIRLINE-SECURITY measures could ruin photographic film in checked baggage, the Eastman Kodak Co. warns. Some antihijacking devices used to check baggage for possible concealed weapons utilize X rays, which will "fog" photographic film. One of the best ways to protect film while traveling is to place it in a strong, clear, plastic bag and hand-carry it. Even though the film may be clearly visible in the bag, make sure that airline boarding personnel and customs officials are aware of the film so that it isn't accidentally subjected to X rays.

PRIVATE CLUBS organized for social and recreational use by members will not lose their exemption from Federal income-tax liability by making their facilities available at no more than cost to charitable organizations for fund-raising purposes, the Internal Revenue Service has ruled.

LEATHER GLOVES in need of washing may look and feel better if you use a hair shampoo or soap containing lanolin.

Buying Burial Plots

SOONER or later nearly everyone will become involved in choosing a cemetery lot. It may be an emotional not-very-rational experience precipitated by the unexpected death of a close relative. It may be the result of high-pressure selling by telephone or door-to-door salesmen. Or it may be a dispassionate choice begun in one's own behalf while in good health, either to try to ensure burial in a place of one's choosing or to spare next-of-kin from having to make the decision.

Whatever the circumstances, problems almost always arise. The careful decision made by a man in good health may look like an expensive mistake to his survivors if death should come, say, two employers later when the family is living a half-a-continent or so away from the burial plot. An emotion-ridden decision at time of death may result in a larger-than-necessary expenditure. And dealings with high-pressure salesmen compound grief when, as sometimes happens, it is discovered that the deceased or his kin had been bilked by paying for a lot of funeral services that proved not to be available when death came.

An executive of the American Cemetery Association in Columbus, Ohio, advocates the purchase of lots "when the pressure of grief is not there." He says the advantages of a careful, rational act and the comfort of owning a lot will outweigh any inconvenience if the lot happens to be far away from a person's home at the time of his death.

But don't underestimate the possible inconvenience and cost. It begins at the time of death. Usually it is necessary to engage the services of two funeral directors when a body must be transported for some distance, one at the place of death and one at the place of burial. Probably this will add at least $100 to funeral and burial costs.

Shipment of a body for long distances is expensive. It costs more than $300 to send a body by air, now the most feasible method, from coast to coast.

Add to all this the cost of transportation for family members who attend the burial. And there will be subsequent travel costs if family members wish to visit the grave.

Advance purchase of a cemetery lot does not necessarily guarantee burial in it. Although state laws vary, many give the ultimate right of decision on funeral and burial details to the widow or next-of-kin. Thus a person who wishes to be buried in a certain place regardless of costs should make sure his family knows of this desire.

Cemetery-lot salesmen often push advance purchase as a way to beat rising costs of lots. Prices have unquestionably been going up. But so have interest rates and money invested in, say, a savings-and-loan account or bonds instead of a cemetery lot likely will return in interest far more than enough to cover any increase in the price of a cemetery lot.

Persons who see more advantages than disadvantages in before-death purchase of a cemetery lot should take the initiative in seeking out a site.

Some cemeteries are run for profit; others are operated on a nonprofit basis by such groups as churches or fraternal organizations. Whatever the type of operation, check carefully on the reputation of the owners and managers.

Make sure you understand what care and maintenance services for grave sites and cemetery grounds are and are not covered by the price of a lot. Some cemetery managements boast that they provide "perpetual care." This means little unless the management makes a commitment to set aside periodically a portion of its income in a fund, often a trust fund administered by a third party such as a bank, to ensure that money always will be available to meet maintenance costs.

A person who wants to minimize the selection problem for his survivors without a before-death lot purchase should take the same sort of initiative and make the same careful checks. He can then tell members of his immediate family of his cemetery preferences in order. Or he can write down his preferences and tell his family where they can be found upon his death.

THE IMMEDIATE KIN of U.S. war dead who are buried overseas can get free passports for travel to visit the graves of the victims. The American Battle Monuments Commission, Washington, D.C. 20315, will provide letters authorizing the free passports. The commission also will provide friends and relatives of war dead with precise location of graves, information on best routes of travel to cemeteries and on room accommodations in the vicinity, and photographs of headstones or sections of memorial tablets on which the names of missing servicemen are engraved.

MANY PERSONS WHO COLLAPSED while eating have died unnecessarily because friends, bystanders, or even physicians assumed incorrectly that they were having a heart attack when actually they were choking on food, according to the National Safety Council. Quick action is necessary to save a choking victim. The lodged food should be pulled from his throat if possible. There are estimates that in about 50 per cent of such cases, food will still be on the tongue, at the top of the air passage and within reach of the fingers.

Vital Records for New Widows

FEW men outlive their wives. In recognition of this vital statistic, many older men are careful to keep their wives advised on the status of life insurance, investments, home mortgages, and other matters that would be of great importance to a new widow. Younger men, less aware that they are likely to die before their wives, often fail to keep their wives informed on such matters. The oversight can compound a widow's grief.

One of the best ways to minimize a new widow's problems is to list and periodically revise important information she should have immediately at hand. Either give her the list or make sure she knows where it is located. Following is a checklist of items that should be included:

✔ A recapitulation of insurance in force and where the policies are located. Many insurance agents, on request, will prepare a recapitulation. The recapitulation should show policy number, face value, any provision for double indemnity or other special benefit in event of accidental death, name of beneficiary, and whether the value of any policy has been reduced by borrowing against it.

✔ A statement of whether a will has been prepared and, if so, its location.

✔ The name, address, and telephone number of the husband's lawyer if he has one.

✔ The precise location of a cemetery lot, if one has

been purchased, and the location of documents proving ownership.

✓ Husband's and wife's Social Security numbers and the address of the nearest Social Security office.

✓ Brief description of any retirement plans in which the husband has participated and the benefits, if any, that may be payable to a widow. Note the location of any papers detailing the retirement plan.

✓ Veterans of military service should advise their wives to check with the Veterans Administration on possible eligibility for benefits including a burial allowance, education assistance for widow and children, pensions, and dependency and indemnity allowances.

✓ Note the location of military discharge papers, military serial number, and, if one was assigned, Veterans Administration claim or C number.

✓ Location of marriage certificate and any birth certificates that have been obtained for any member of the family.

✓ A recapitulation of any stocks and bonds, including their location and their value when acquired.

✓ The location of automobile titles. If money is still owed on a car, note the amount of payments, how often they are due, when the car is scheduled to be paid for, and the name and address of the holder of the car note. Many car financing deals include insurance that pays any balance due if the debtor dies; double check and note it if you have such a policy.

✓ If you are a homeowner, note the location of the title to the property. If the house is mortgaged, note the name and address of the mortgage holder, the location of mortgage payment books or receipts, amount and frequency of mortgage payment, and when payments should be completed. Be sure to note if you have an in-

surance policy that would pay off the mortgage if you
die.

✔ The location and number of any checking or
savings accounts in banks or savings-and-loan institutions.

✔ The locations of any safety deposit boxes that
have been rented.

✔ A recapitulation of any sizable outstanding
debts, including the amounts and the names of the
creditors.

✔ Any preference for the handling of your remains and whether there has been any advance arrangement for donation of organs.

There is a simple test to determine whether you
should prepare such a list: How many of the things in
the list above that seem important to you would your
wife know about if you were to die when you lay this
book down?

FRUIT TREES advertised as bearing five fruits such as
peaches, plums, and cherries should be regarded with caution.
The Council of Better Business Bureaus, Inc., says that highly
trained growers can sometimes successfully bud or graft five
fruit species to one root stock but that the average homeowner
has negligible chances of producing more than three species.
Any multiple-species venture, the CBBB suggests, should be
regarded as an educational rather than a fruit-producing venture.
Multi-species trees should not be confused with trees producing
several varieties of one fruit. Chances of success with the latter
are much better.

BALLPOINT INK STAINS on washable clothing often
will disappear if rubbed with petroleum jelly and then washed
with hot water and a detergent.

New Rules for
Moving Companies

ALARMED at the rate of "frustration and disappointment" created by household-goods movers who have "failed to match their promises with performance," the Interstate Commerce Commission (ICC) has clamped new, tougher regulations on interstate moving companies.

The ICC says its new rules "are intended to create an atmosphere of full disclosure (of information) between the mover and the householder" and to "minimize the increasing consumer-carrier frictions."

The regulations are specific and detailed, but in general they provide for the first time:

✔ Movers must tell the householder if they cannot pickup or deliver his goods on the date or within the period of time agreed on. The carrier must notify the householder of the delay "at least 24 hours before the last requested delivery date," and he is prohibited from giving false or misleading reasons for the delay.

✔ Carriers must give a cost estimate if the shipper asks for it. The estimate must be presented on a standard form to facilitate comparing the estimate of one company with those of others. Estimates must contain a statement of the maximum amount of money the householder will have to pay at the time his furniture is delivered. In practice, this will mean that if the carrier underestimates charges, he cannot demand on delivery more than 110 per cent of the estimated cost. Thus, should the carrier estimate costs at $600, the shipper knows he cannot be expected to pay more than $660 on delivery. He must eventually pay the full amount on any charges beyond the 110 per cent figure. At present, carriers can and do refuse to unload unless paid in full upon delivery, though the price may be more than the mover estimated.

✔ Movers may not print statements on delivery receipts purporting to release the carrier from liability for damages. Carriers also must periodically report to the ICC the status of all damage and loss suits against them and if the processing of claims has been delayed, they must explain why. Formerly carriers had to report only specified kinds of damage and loss claims.

✔ Carriers must give shippers "orders for service," which are documents containing such details as special services for packaging fragile items, location of the scale to be used in weighing the shipment, and name, address, and telephone number of the mover's agent who will handle unloading at the destination.

✔ Movers must state on bills of lading, which are the receipts for goods and the contracts of carriage, the agreed dates or periods for delivery and pickup, estimate of charges, the maximum amount of money that can be demanded on delivery, and the weight of the truck before loading.

✔ Carriers must let shippers witness the weighing of moving trucks, both empty and loaded, if the shipper so desires. The weight of household goods is determined for billing purposes, by weighing the truck before and after loading rather than by weighing individual items.

✔ Movers also must give householders a revised ICC booklet titled "Summary of Information for Shippers of Household Goods."

Moving Yourself

A HOUSEHOLD move, almost always a difficult undertaking, can be particularly unpleasant in the summer. Pickups and deliveries are more likely to be delayed then because the demand on moving companies is at a peak. Damage to furniture is greater because many unskilled workers are temporarily employed as movers. One way to minimize such problems, and save a substantial bit of money too, is to move yourself.

Rental trailers and van trucks in wide variety are now available on a rent-it-here, leave-it-there basis. But before attempting a major do-it-yourself move, consider several factors carefully

Are you or members of your family physically up to carrying your heaviest furniture in and out of houses? If not, do you have friends willing and able to help out or is a source of hired help available at both ends of the move? If you don't have adequate help, perhaps the job should be left to the professionals.

If you have many pieces of furniture or a number of unusually heavy pieces, go slow on attempting a do-it-yourself move.

And before committing yourself to a move, make a careful estimate of the weight and volume of your belongings. A booklet, "Moving Guide," which contains estimating tables, is available free from U-Haul rental agencies or from the U-Haul Rental System, 2727 N. Central Ave., Room 600, Phoenix, Ariz. 85004. When you have made your estimate, determine how large a trailer or truck will be needed to haul your belongings. Rental companies should be able to give you the capacities of various sizes of van-type trucks and trailers.

If you need a large trailer, is your car up to towing it? If you need a truck to make the move, be sure you or whoever might drive it can handle the vehicle. If you have doubts, ask the rental company to let you try driving the truck before you commit yourself to renting it.

The savings in a do-it-yourself move are considerable. A commercial van line, invoking Government-set rates on interstate moves, will charge about $1,000 to move 5,000 pounds from coast to coast. You can move the same amount the same distance in a 16-foot rented truck for around $600. Savings are less for shorter moves and lighter loads.

In shopping for rental vehicles, make sure that you understand clearly what is included in the rental charges. What liability insurance protection is provided? Is insurance on your furniture included?

With some companies and on moves to certain areas at certain times of the year, you may have to pay an extra "drop-off" charge for a one-way rental. The charges vary from about $50 to $200. Nearly all companies, for example, levy a drop charge on one-way rentals to Florida in the winter, when moves into the state far exceed moves out.

Companies usually quote a basic flat rate by the week, day, or hour for trucks. These vary with the length of the vehicle. Add to the flat rate a sales tax if one prevails in your state, a deposit, and collision insurance up to the $200 or $250 deductible the company carries on the truck.

Costs of a move from Seattle to Washington, D.C., in a 16-foot U-Haul van truck, for example, would include: $457.50 rental for 2,783 miles and 11 days; collision insurance of $2 a day or $10 a week; and a $40 deposit and sales tax, all payable in advance. Mileage in excess of the 2,783-mile base would cost 14 cents a mile extra; you would get a refund, however, if actual mileage was less than the base. You would have to pay for gasoline, which could cost more than $150 for such a move. Hertz and Avis have roughly comparable charges.

Gas consumption must be figured at a considerably higher rate than for the average car. Rental companies estimate that their trucks average anywhere from 6 to 10 miles per gallon. Some companies charge a higher mileage fee and reimburse you for gasoline purchases.

Rental trailers are cheaper than trucks but less advisable for long hauls with heavy loads. Drivers should take into consideration the additional wear and tear on automobiles and allow for greatly reduced gas mileage. A 6-by-14-foot trailer, for example, which will hold three to four rooms of furniture, may be too heavy for a six-cylinder car. Tell the rental agency what kind of car you have when you talk sizes and prices.

Unless a driver is accustomed to pulling a camp or horse trailer, hauling a load of furniture may present problems, especially in parking.

GI INSURANCE owners whose policies are for renewable five-year term insurance face a stiff premium increase if they renew their policies for another five-year segment after age 50. The problem is faced by many veterans since the average age of a World War II veteran is now more than 50 years. One way to ease the payment problem is to convert to modified life. The monthly premium for a $10,000 policy will then remain constant at about $16. However, at age 65 the face value of the policy decreases by one-half unless the owner at that time elects to begin paying a monthly premium of approximately $42. Other policy conversions are possible; details are available at Veterans Administration offices.

Wigs Aren't Always
What They Seem

THE synthetic wig market is relatively new, growing rapidly, and as it grows, it becomes increasingly confusing to prospective customers.

With new manufacturing processes and changing fashion, there has developed a widening difference in prices, which now are between $8 and $179 for women's wigs that may appear to be quite similar when styled and worn. The customer may well wonder what the differences are.

The popular advantages of synthetic wigs over human hair wigs are several: They are much less expensive; they can be washed and worn without the expensive professional restyling required by human hair wigs; and they are much more resistant to wet and damp weather.

The main factors to consider before buying a synthetic wig are fiber, construction, and style. However, at least as important to a wig's wearability is the care it receives after purchase.

The least of the prospective buyer's worries is the fiber. There are many wig factories, but only a few fiber manufacturers. So most wigmakers get their fiber from the same places.

With only rare exceptions, synthetic wigs are made of a type of fiber called modacrylic. The two predominant brands of modacrylic fiber are Dynel, manufactured by Union Carbide, and a Japanese-made fiber called Kanekalon. Some wigs are a mixture of several quality grades of the same fiber or of two different brands of fiber.

All modacrylic fibers will have similar properties of durability. However, wigmakers sometimes treat the fiber to alter its appearance or texture slightly. There are only slight differences between Kanekalon and Dynel, which are the materials used in most wigs on the market.

Kanekalon is not usually as shiny as Dynel and is slightly more expensive. The price difference in a finished wig should not be more than one or two dollars, however. The gloss of Dynel may be a disadvantage in some colors, as it often is in light brown, but an advantage in others.

The most important difference in wigs, governing price, fit, and style, is the way they are constructed. Almost all wigs are manufactured outside the United States, since labor costs are the major price factor. There are three major types of construction:

Machine-sewn wefted: This is the most common type of synthetic wig, and its cost runs from the least expensive to about $55. The fiber is connected to a continuous strip (weft) usually sewn in a spiral into the cap of the wig. The fibers face one direction, and can be combed in only that direction. Such wigs must completely cover the user's own hairline.

Hand-tied wigs: Each fiber is tied individually into the cap, and the hair is distributed all over the cap. Hair strands may be single- or double-knotted, the latter being more expensive and stronger. Prices range higher than for the machine-sewn type, but a hand-tied wig can usually be obtained for between $30 and $40. The advantages are that the fiber can be combed in any direction, making it more versatile in styling; also, the cap is lighter weight.

Combinations: For off-the-face styles or "natural-parted" wigs, machine-sewn wigs have some sections that are hand tied. A hand-tied front enables the hair to be combed both forward and away from the face, so the wearer can choose an off-the-face style in which she combs her own hair over the front of the wig.

A natural-part-wig is made by the use of a hand-tied section at the location of the part. The combination wigs may sell for up to $70 for the best quality, but can usually be found for prices about $5 to $15 higher than all-machine-sewn wigs.

Machine-crocheted: The most expensive synthetic wigs are made by Reid-Meredith, machine-crocheted wigs which sell for between $60 and $179. The process is exclusive, and the wigs are manufactured entirely in the United States. Examination of the wig cap shows the same all-over distribution of fiber and the lighter weight of the hand-tied wig. Also, the hair can be combed in any direction, and is firmly secured in the cap.

Here are a few things to check in buying a wig:

Evenness of the construction. Wefts should be sewn in evenly, and at the origin or center the hair should not fall away conspicuously. In a hand-tied wig, be sure there are no bald spots. However, a greater concentration of fiber on one side or in front may be part of the style for which the wig is designed.

Make sure that you can handle the wig yourself. Try on several and try your hand at styling them. The shop's stylist can be of help, but you should be able to make the wig look good by yourself.

Make sure the cap fits comfortably. If the cap is too snug, it may "creep" up when worn.

Once the wig is purchased, care is important. But the advice the buyer receives will vary considerably. It goes like this:

Washing. Synthetic wigs should be washed in cold water—never warm or hot—and allowed to dry naturally for about 24 hours away from any source of heat. There are three choices suggested in soap: baby shampoo, a mild cold-water soap such as Woolite, or a cleaning agent designed just for synthetic wigs. Some wig sellers say the cold-water soaps can be bad for the wig, others prefer them to baby shampoo, saying even baby shampoo can be drying. The very cautious wig owner might want to use the products designed just for synthetic wigs, which often include a conditioner. The wig should be washed about every 24 wearings, or when it appears to need it. If a wig appears to be too shiny, try dusting it lightly with talcum powder and brushing it. This will cut down the sheen.

Heat. Wig sellers are unanimous that the synthetics should never be exposed to any source of artificial heat, such as an open oven, hot water, radiator, or hair dryer. But they divide on the matter of the sun. Wearing a wig during prolonged sunbathing may cause it to frizz, some say. Others contend the sun should not have any effect.

BIG-CITY VISITORS should carry plenty of change and one-dollar bills. City transit systems in growing numbers are requiring passengers to have exact fares to board buses. Many cab drivers carry no more than $5 in change. Both bus and cab fares are deposited by drivers in locked strong-boxes to which they have no keys. The fare requirements have been instituted in an effort to decrease the robberies and murders of drivers by eliminating or sharply reducing the amount of cash a holdup man might get.

Picking Diamonds

SHOPPING for diamonds is no easier than paying for them. Prices vary widely, depending on many factors.

The first rule to follow in choosing a diamond is to deal with a reputable jeweler. Then you should consider various diamond characteristics.

A diamond reflects many colors so be sure you know the color of the diamond itself, which best reveals itself in natural light. Blue-white diamonds are desirable but almost impossible to find. Crystal-clear diamonds are more readily available.

The way a diamond is displayed affects its apparent color. Blue walls or lights in a jewelry store tend to make the gem look better than it actually may be.

Yellow or brown in a diamond reduce its value; any grease on a diamond reflects these colors strongly. An unscrupulous dealer may treat a yellow diamond with a purple substance that will make the gem look clear until you wash it. And if you are trying to sell or trade a diamond, he may casually brush it against his hair so that it will pick up grease and look its poorest.

Cracks and other flaws, like traces of minerals, are not always undesirable in a diamond, according to one professional gemmologist. Flaws can give a diamond character, he says, and aid in identification if it is ever stolen.

"An absolutely colorless diamond is worth more

with a small flaw than a flawless diamond with the faintest tint of yellow or brown," he adds.

The weight of a diamond is measured in carats and points: 100 points make a carat and it takes about 143 carats to equal an ounce.

If all other characteristics are equal, cost will increase with the weight of a diamond and, after the three-carat level, cost tends to increase faster than weight.

Proportioning or the ratio of the top portion of a diamond to the bottom portion, where the diameter decreases, affects the angles of the diamond's planes and hence influences brilliance. Ideally, the top or crown should be about one-fourth of the total depth of the diamond, though a slightly larger crown may improve brilliance.

Diamonds, like their wearers, come in round, elliptical, pear, and other shapes. Odd-shaped diamonds are in demand today and tend to be higher priced than round diamonds. But shape is a matter of taste and not an indication of the quality of a diamond.

CRYSTAL-CHANDELIER cleaning, usually a tedious task involving the removal of individual crystals, is made easier with a new aerosol spray introduced by the Herbert Stanley Co., 8140 N. Ridgeway, Skokie, Ill. 60076. Old newspapers are spread beneath a chandelier and then the product, called Wieman Chandelier Rinse, is sprayed liberally on the chandelier frame and crystals. The compound, which has a suggested retail price of $3, carries away much grime and dust as it drips off. Though the cleaner will improve a chandelier's appearance, it is not as effective as hand cleaning and polishing. Electricity should be turned off when using the compound and not turned on until the chandelier is thoroughly dry.

**If you enjoyed this book,
you will also like . . .**

THE CONSUMER'S HANDBOOK
(first edition)

Finding a Suitable Fund
On Driving Cool
Learning a Language
Rug Cleaning: Dos and Don'ts
How to Save on Gasoline
Shopping for Good Health
Getting the Most Out of Color TV
On Selling Your House
Check Your Home Insurance
What's New in Golf?
Ice Cream: Good and Bad
How to Read a Prospectus
New Wrinkles in Sailing
How to Select Your Dentist
How to Pick a Good Fur
Wigs for Everyone
Fertilizers: What's the Difference?
How to Buy Binoculars
Keeping Burglars Away
How to Choose a Lawyer
Hearing Aids for Children
Easy-to-Use Cameras
Cutting Camera Costs
Picking a Suitable Scotch
How to Select an Appraiser
Caring for Your Battery
The Costs of Quick Cash
Premixed Cocktails: Any Good?

How to Buy Appliances
Selecting a Physician
How to Buy Antiques
Checking a Dream House
How to Prevent Being Gypped
Testing the Twin-XX-Twenty
Should You Join an Auto Club
Does It Pay to Reupholster?
Going Camping in Style
Advantages of a Built-In Vacuum
Going Abroad? Skip Kennedy
If Your Tax Return Is Questioned
How to Find a Tree Surgeon
How to Become an Investor
Keeping Immune from Disease
On Cooling the House
How to Rent Furniture
How to Buy Ski Equipment
New Tacks in Sailing
Choosing the Right Paint
Should You Lease Your Car?
How to Shop for a Sauna
Caring for Your Silver
On Safe Cleaning of Fabrics
Storing Your Garden Equipment
How to Take Your Pet Traveling
Tips on Buying Land by Mail
plus many more "how-to" tips

Published July, 1969; 162 pages; $1.85
available from
DOW JONES BOOKS, P.O. BOX 300, PRINCETON, NEW JERSEY 08540

3868